RECOVERING OUTREACH
Concepts, issues and practices

RECOVERING OUTREACH

Concepts, issues and practices

Veronica McGivney

NIACE

THE NATIONAL ORGANISATION
FOR ADULT LEARNING

Published by the National Institute of
Adult Continuing Education (England and Wales)

21 De Montfort Street
Leicester LE1 7GE
Company registration no. 2603322
Charity registration no. 1002775

First published 2000

NIACE, the national organisation for adult learning,
has a broad remit to promote lifelong learning
opportunities for adults. NIACE works to develop
increased participation in education and training,
particularly for those who do not have easy access
because of barriers of class, gender, age, race,
language and culture, learning difficulties and
disabilities, or insufficient financial resources.

NIACE's website on the Internet is http://www.niace.org.uk

Cataloguing in Publication Data
A CIP record of this title is available from the British Library

Designed and typeset by Boldface
Printed in Great Britain by Alden Press
ISBN: 1 86201 099 4

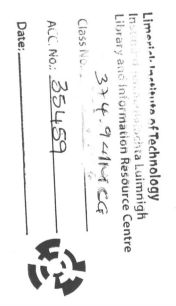

Contents

Acknowledgements

A number of people provided literature, information and contacts for this study, and other took the time to discuss outreach strategies and relevant issues with me. Thanks are due to all of the following:

Jon Boagey, National Youth Agency
Alan Clarke, NIACE
John Cope, Knowsley Community College
Jim Cowan, FEFCW
Kellam Dale, BBC Education
Julia Dinsdale, Widening Participation project at City University, the University of East London, London Guildhall University, University of North London, the Open University in London, Queen Mary and Westfield College
Lyn Eaton, Knowsley Community College
Ed Ellis, New College Southampton
Toni Fazaeli, FEFC
Jean Flynn, Knowsley Community College
Linsey Fraser, University of Leeds
Michael Freeston, WEA
Trevor Gordon, Lambeth College
Peter Harrison, Oaklands College
Peter Lavender, NIACE
Heather Jackson, BBC Education
Alan Maw, Knowsley Community College
Anne McKeown, North East London College
Bryan Merton, NIACE
Fiona O'Brien, BBC Education
Mark Ravenhall, East Sussex County Council
Jim Soulsby, NIACE
Alan Tuckett, NIACE
Cheryl Turner, NIACE
Merillie Vaughan Huxley, FEFC
Angela Wood, Oxford LEA

Introduction

Adult learning surveys show with depressing regularity that there is a clear and persisting socio-economic and socio-cultural divide between the people who engage in organised education and training programmes and those who do not. The recent NIACE/RSGB (Research Surveys of Great Britain) survey of a weighted sample of 4,091 adults showed that social class remains a powerful influence on participation and that although rates have risen since 1999, the sharpest rise is among professional and managerial groups (NIACE, 2000). For a raft of reasons that have been mulled over for some years, many people shun organised forms of learning, especially when they are delivered in dedicated centres and institutions which, however relaxed and informal they may be on the inside, can appear intimidating and exclusive to those who have had less than happy school experiences or who belong to segments of the population who traditionally do not participate in any forms of post-compulsory education or training.

It is a commonplace that people on the lowest incomes make up a high proportion of those who do not participate in organised learning programmes. Yet, as illustrated in a transnational project (OECD, 1999), learning can make a significant contribution towards combating social and economic disadvantage. In the project report, *Overcoming Exclusion through Adult Learning*, social exclusion is defined as something that is more than just material deprivation. Families and communities may be 'materially poor but socially rich': the most excluded groups are those who suffer both material hardship *and* subsequent breakdown or loss of extended family and social networks. The report confirms what many people working with adults have long known: that informal, locally-based and locally-inspired approaches can be more effective at promoting engagement in learning among such groups than mainstream provision in education institutions, and they often have a more wide-ranging impact. However, such initiatives are invariably under-resourced. 'Time and time again the most promising lifelong learning initiatives on the margins of education and employment have suffered the chronic insecurity of under-funding' (Nash, 1999).

This comment sums up the frustration of countless adult educators in the UK. Over the past three or four decades, there has been a plethora of attempts to develop alternative, locally-based learning approaches with groups who are under-represented in formal education provision, especially those disadvantaged by factors such as poverty, race, gender, age and disability. Short-term community-based projects and initiatives have come and gone in rapid succession. Although many have succeeded in attracting people into organised learning activities, few of the methods and approaches that account for their effectiveness have been absorbed into mainstream education and their impact has consequently been short-lived. Many such projects have been caught in a vicious circle: run on small budgets, often by part-time and short-term staff without the time or resources to spend on assessment and evaluation of outcomes, they have been unable to produce statistical evidence of long-term impact. This is frequently used as an excuse for not making sustained investment in this kind of work. Moreover, informal community-based initiatives targeted at under-represented groups were dealt an almost terminal blow by the changes in policy and funding arrangements introduced in the 1992 Further and Higher Education Act. Since then it has been a major problem to justify public expenditure on time- and labour-intensive outreach approaches which may initially involve small numbers and which do not produce rapid and easily measurable outcomes. This situation is not confined to Britain. International studies have found that few post-compulsory education funding systems are flexible enough to take into account the time-lag between paying costs and realising benefits that often occurs in work with new groups of learners:

> *(Lifelong learning) is undertaken at a particular time…and the benefits are reaped later. This creates difficulties where capital markets or other institutional arrangements, such as public budgeting practices, do not allow the comparison of costs and benefits across time periods. It has the effect of squeezing out lifelong learning activities that do not produce benefits quickly and, by implication, rationing lifelong learning opportunities to those individuals who are likely to demonstrate the desired benefits most quickly, or who are capable of financing the costs on their own.* (OECD, 1996: 239)

In Britain the result of this, as Uden (1996) has argued, is that although we have long had the experience and ability to widen participation in education and training, we have not taken full advantage of them. Now, however, the pendulum is swinging back towards the reclamation and redevelopment of the skills required to engage new groups in learning. Insights into widening participation that have been around for several decades have resurfaced in a series of influential national reports such as Kennedy (1997), Fryer (1997) and the Policy Action Team on Skills (DfEE, 1999b), and these are being taken on board by the current government. For the first time in some years, there is recognition at ministerial level of the diversity of adult learning requirements and the need for a corresponding diversity of forms of, and contexts for, learning. A succession of policy and funding initiatives since 1997 reflect a genuine concern to engage people who have missed out on, or been failed by, education in the past, and there is now acceptance that the creation of a lifelong learning culture will require the development of community-based learning opportunities and collaboration with other services and agencies in combating economic and social disadvantage

By working locally and providing learning activities in familiar and non-threatening local venues, education providers can succeed in widening participation among new segments of the population. But this kind of work, which is often referred to as 'outreach', requires a substantial investment of time and resources and the deployment of people with the appropriate networking and trust-building skills. It is not an easy option and the results may take a while to appear. But it is essential if there is a genuine desire to make learning opportunities more accessible to a wider mix of people. In view of this, it seemed timely to undertake a study which explored the nature and meaning of outreach in relation to widening participation, and considered whether some of the lessons gained from outreach approaches in the past still have relevance today. The study was funded by the Department for Education and Employment and was conducted between September 1999 and March 2000.

Aims

The principal aims of the study were:

- to explore the role of outreach in post-16 educational provision and practice
- to identify the kinds of outreach approaches and strategies currently being used to widen participation
- to identify the role of outreach in widening participation in learning.

These areas were explored through a review of existing research and other written information, and interviews with staff in institutions and organisations with well-developed outreach strategies or which had conducted relevant studies. Those which were visited or which provided written information included two local education authorities, four further education colleges, two (pre-'92) universities and a consortium of mainly newer higher education institutions, the WEA, the FEFC in England and Wales, the National Youth Agency and BBC Education.

Discussions with staff in these organisations and other individuals working in the field of adult education centred on:

- the different concepts and definitions of outreach used
- the kinds of outreach strategies employed
- the costs and funding of outreach activities
- the skills, status and conditions of service of outreach workers
- the impact and outcomes of outreach activities (for learners, target groups, the wider community and providers)

- the kinds of issues that arise in doing outreach
- the views and perceptions of practitioners.

A list of the people who provided information and contacts and those with whom discussions were held is provided in the Acknowledgements section.

The report

The report is not based on a case-study approach as this has already been done effectively for the DfEE demonstration projects (Watson and Tyers, 1998); nor is it simply a good practice guide as this has also been produced by Watson and Tyers (1998) and Wood (forthcoming). Rather it is an attempt to explore, in relation to past and current practice, the different understandings of outreach; its role in widening participation among people under-represented in organised education; the implications of doing outreach and the range of practical and ethical considerations involved.

Unattributed quotations are from the people who were interviewed during the course of this study. For reasons of confidentiality, only the sector they work in is identified.

While the study was supported by the DfEE, all conclusions and observations are the author's own.

Origins and meanings

In its simplest sense of reaching out or taking services to groups and individuals, outreach is a method that has long been employed in a number of sectors – in youth and community work; in the pastoral and missionary work of different religions (Woking Mosque, for example, has run a 'Benefits Roadshow' for Pakistani families); in health work (for example, health visitors) and drug-related work; in community education and other public services (public libraries commonly take services to rural and isolated areas, hospitals and day centres for the elderly, and some work with schools and different community groups and organisations). Outreach is also commonly used in an international development context (for example, in literacy and health interventions, 'barefoot doctors', and so on) although the actual word may not be used in that context.

There are different accounts of the origins of outreach. It has variously been seen as having started in missionary work – a reaching out from centres of Christianity to unbelievers (Clancy and Stuart, 1995); in the philanthropic, community-spirited activities conducted in deprived areas of London in the mid-nineteenth century (Rhodes and Stimson, 1994), and in the late nineteenth-century attempts to extend a learning culture to a wider population through university extension work, extra-mural classes and university settlements (Fordham *et al*, 1979). Some youth service workers, however, see outreach as a more recent development which originated in the USA in the late 1950s as a response to the problems of street gangs:

These hip young tearaways shunned established youth work services in favour of street corners and pool halls. As the gangs moved underground, youth workers had to follow them into their subterranean world if they were to keep in contact with them and ultimately control them. This style of outreach came to Britain in the 1960s at a time when our own gangs of mods and rockers were shunning church-run youth clubs in favour of coffee bars, nightclubs and bank holiday showdowns. British youth workers responded to this situation by establishing their own coffee bars where these young rebels could smoke cigarettes, listen to their favourite music, drink subsidised coffee and maintain their street image. This new relaxed approach which accepted, and worked within, new youth cultures was expanded into detached work. Youth workers moved out of their drop-ins and on to the street to contact young people and offer their services.
(Gilman, 1992: 6)

Some adult and community education workers prefer to locate the origins of educational outreach in the radical community-based work developed in the 1960s-70s by university adult educators in and around cities such as Liverpool and Southampton. These aimed to engage with particular communities on their own terms, to explore with them issues of immediate and local concern and to jointly develop appropriate solutions (Mace, 1992; Stuart and Thomson, 1995). Other institutions and education providers were prompted to work in similar ways and, between the 1970s and the 1980s, spurred on by the influential Russell Report (1973), a range of community-based learning programmes were targeted specifically at women, working-class and ethnic minority communities alongside efforts to make post-16 education institutions more accessible. In the Inner London Education Authority (ILEA), for example, a working party was set up after the evidence it provided for the Russell enquiry revealed stark imbalances in adult participation (Taubman and Cushman, 1981). The working party suggested that educational establishments needed to connect more with their local communities and appoint staff (community education workers) to research local educational needs. The important literacy campaigns launched in the 1970s also involved reaching out to target communities through broadcasts and outreach working.

These developments reflected growing recognition, voiced in the Russell Report, that significant sections of the population were not gaining access to organised adult education provision and that there was a need to develop locally-based, non-formal learning activities which would be 'more closely related to the expectations and wishes of local people' (Fordham *et al*, 1979). The term 'outreach' was widely applied to such work but it gradually dropped out of common parlance between the late 1980s and early 1990s as the funding changes and instrumental emphasis of Conservative education policies made it increasingly more difficult to implement outreach strategies. Cuts in local authority spending and the changes brought about by the 1992 Further and Higher Education Act led to the loss not only of a substantial amount of outreach work (except in areas of the curriculum such as basic skills), but also of many of the practitioners skilled in doing it:

> *12 years ago before they killed community education, the LEA had a good tradition of doing outreach community work.* (LEA officer)

> *Outreach went out of fashion and was significantly reduced as a direct result of the 1992 FHE Act because of the organisational and funding changes the Act introduced. The FEFC rewarded the throughput of students. Both colleges and local authorities found it hard to fund outreach when it was easier to secure funding by going after 'safer' students.* (Wood, 1999)

A similar reduction of outreach activity occurred in higher education. Many pre-1992 universities used to provide outreach programmes, often in collaboration with partners such as the WEA, as part of the extramural work of their continuing education (and sometimes other) departments. Some institutions such as the University of Leeds still have a strong tradition of community-based work and delivery. On the whole, however, this has tended to be relatively small scale and marginal to the main work of the institution, and with the advent of mainstreaming in 1992, much of this kind of work changed significantly. A number of continuing education departments underwent restructuring and there was a noticeable reduction in locally-based activities. As a result:

> *The knowledge base of the institution is less accessible to its communities than was previously the case. The institution in turn has lost access to the knowledge and experience of such communities which it previously received through staff engaged in day schools, residential and short course programmes, and community-based action research.* (McNair, 1999: 58-59)

Steele (1999: 104) relates how, during the period of resource-starved expansion in the late 1980s and early 1990s, many of the higher education institutions which had traditionally been concerned with delivering less formal education in the community found it increasingly difficult to provide:

> *Government policy has dragged university adult education (now called continuing education) into the mainstream, professionalised it and refocused it away from its extra-mural origins to the internal institutional needs of the universities....The demise of community education in the local authorities is leaving a vacuum which now threatens the partnership with universities, and Access schemes, painfully developed over 20 years, have to scramble for funds or have already been scrapped.*

Now, however, there has been a resurgence of interest in outreach working, although the actual term may not always be used. A series of influential reports and a succession of policy and funding initiatives since 1997 have encouraged a return to some of the methods and practices used in earlier years to reach and work with the groups least represented in formal education. Among these one may note (not necessarily in this order):

- the 'Kennedy Report' (1997)
- the 'Fryer report' (1997)
- the Green Paper (DfEE, 1998a) *The Learning Age: A Renaissance for a New Britain*;
- the establishment of the Social Exclusion Unit and its subsequent report on neighbourhood renewal (1999) *Bringing Britain Together: a national strategy for neighbourhood renewal*;
- the setting up of employment, education and health action zones;
- the establishment of 100 Lifelong Learning partnerships with the role of

reaching out into local communities, identifying local learning needs and acting as a forum for delivering lifelong learning;

- the launch of the Adult and Community Learning Fund;
- the introduction of New Deal for Communities with a role to improve employment, housing and education, foster community spirit and harness the active involvement of the local communities;
- the Moser Report on literacy (1999) and the establishment of the Basic Skills Community Fund;
- the launch of the Neighbourhood Support Fund targeted at young people in areas of deprivation and involving local community organisations;
- the report of the Policy Action Team on Skills (DfEE, 1999a) *Skills for neighbourhood renewal: local solutions*;
- the White Paper *Learning to Succeed – a new framework for post-16 learning* (DfEE, 1999c) and subsequent Learning and Skills Bill Prospectus (DfEE, 1999b; 1999c);
- the establishment of the first 68 trial learndirect (University for Industry) centres in venues such as football clubs, community centres, shopping centres and pubs;
- the launch of the Capital Modernisation Fund with the goal of establishing new ICT learning centres in disadvantaged communities and small businesses;
- the creation of the New Opportunities Fund (NOF) (a National Lottery fund to distribute grants for sustainable projects related to health, education and the environment, and targeted at the most disadvantaged;
- the Community Access to Lifelong Learning (CALL) programme to help develop a nationwide network of learning centres with ICT access to information and learning, with priority given to locally-based projects including development and outreach work for the socially excluded;
- the introduction of the Community Champions Fund, to encourage people to become involved in the renewal of their communities;
- the launch of the Council for Citizenship and Learning in the Community to provide a focus for institutions already assessing community work;
- the introduction of FEFC funding for innovative pilot Non-Schedule 2 projects for adults without qualifications and with basic skills needs.

The key reports and policy documents on lifelong learning that have been produced in the last three years are lavishly sprinkled with references to the importance of working locally with excluded groups and communities, demonstrating that this is a key dimension of the government's linked anti-poverty, community regeneration and lifelong learning strategies. There is a striking commonality of language in the documents. The Adult and Community Learning Fund prospectus (1998b: 3), for example, states that it aims to support: 'activities that will take learning into new sectors of the community not reached by traditional education organisations, providing opportunities that are relevant to the people involved and delivering them in ways that will interest and attract the people who are hardest to reach'.

In its influential final report, the Policy Action Team (PAT) on Skills (DfEE, 1999b) also puts strong emphasis on outreach and first-stage access provision and calls for the development of locally-based, locally-inspired learning activities, in disadvantaged communities:

delivered where people live through neighbourhood learning centres in the management and operation of which local people should, wherever possible, have a significant stake. [These] could take a variety of forms, including FE premises used for outreach work, Lifelong Learning centres as well as local community centres (DfEE, 1999a: 13).

The report notes (p45) that in the areas studied by the Action Team, there was 'often a disturbing lack of connection between educational institutions and some of the local communities they exist to serve'.

The recommendations in the PAT report have been broadly accepted by Government. Work has already started on a strategy for neighbourhood learning centres and the Prospectus for the Learning and Skills Council (DfEE, 1999c: 4.30) declares that:

much more of the right kind of learning will be available in ways that meet the needs of local people, on their own terms and in settings with which they are comfortable....Local learning opportunities, where people learn together in locally-based, familiar environments, provide the key link to learning for individuals of all ages.

According to the Prospectus, the local learning and skills councils will have flexible budgets for, among other things, adult and community learning, pump-priming for small-scale local projects and meeting the needs of people with most difficulty in accessing learning opportunities.

The further and higher education sectors have also been encouraged to do more local and community-based work. There is now a widening participation factor in FE funding, and the strategy, recommended in the Kennedy Report (1997), of allocating extra funding for learners from certain postcode areas was accepted by the Further Education Funding Council for England (FEFCE) and implemented for the first time in 1998-99. A postcode scheme had already been successfully running in the FE sector in Wales, and in the Comprehensive Spending Review letter of guidance to the Further Education Funding Council for Wales (FEFCW) in January 1999, the sector was requested to continue attaching priority to outreach programmes since these were seen to be playing an important part in lifelong learning, community development and regeneration.

Use of postcode weighting has also become part of mainstream higher education funding. There is now a premium paid for students from areas which historically have a low rate of higher education participation, and higher education institutions are expected to widen participation through partnerships and locally-based work. There is also joint HEFC and FEFC funding for work in the community and opening up access to new groups. In *The Learning Age* (DfEE, 1998a: 51), outreach programmes for adults are described as making a 'valuable contribution to lifelong learning' and it is stated that the funding councils and higher education institutions are expected to attach high priority to their continuation.

In Scotland there is a similar emphasis on community-based work. Taking up some of the main proposals in the 1998 report *Communities – Change Through Learning*, the Scottish Office Education and Industry Department distributed a circular on community education to local authorities. This states:

> *Authorities should establish systematic ways of taking into account the views of participants and potential participants in community learning. Reaching and involving non-participants will be essential. The audit and planning process should stimulate communities by extending their awareness of possibilities and needs.* (Circular 4199)

There are, therefore, a number of developments at different stages of planning and development across different sectors and regions that are encouraging the development or expansion of outreach activities (although it is to be noted that this type of work is invariably connected with the notion of 'disadvantage' and widening participation to people in areas of deprivation – a point that will be taken up in a subsequent chapter).

Although the emphasis in current policy on connecting more with local needs has been widely welcomed, as has the recognition of the link between learning and community development, it is not clear that there is a real appreciation of the nature and expense of the outreach work necessary to achieve these objectives. There are several questionable assumptions in policy: first, that sufficient resources will be available to support such activity although, as Chapter 5 will argue, this has rarely been the case; and second, that there are workers with the skills and experience to reach out to and work with different community groups despite signs that many of the staff with the appropriate skills have been lost to the system:

> *I'm very sad that we lost so much that was being done. In 1979 I did all of this. If you're an outside funded project so much is lost because the lessons aren't taken on.* (LEA officer)

> *There's been a massive explosion of all this local stuff but we know less how to do it than we did 20 years ago* (FE manager)

> *We've come round in a complete circle. About 10 years ago we had a lot of outreach activity and outreach centres. Then it all came to a halt. Everything came to this campus. Now it's all coming back again.* (HE staff member)

A third assumption in current policy is that there are common understandings of what is meant by the words 'outreach' and 'community', both of which are frequently mentioned in recent policy documents in relation to widening participation and locally-based learning activities.

Definitions

Like a number of the terms commonly used in post-compulsory education, the word outreach is characterised by conceptual confusion. It tends to be used rather loosely by practitioners and its meaning appears to be taken for granted in much of the literature. For example, the report on DfEE-supported outreach demonstration projects offers no initial definition of outreach, it presumably being implicit both in the location of the work (projects were typically based in particular estates, wards and postcode districts), and in the various aims and approaches described (eg to develop innovative ways of improving access to information and advice on learning opportunities for adults) (Watson and Tyers, 1998).

There is no single and universally accepted definition of 'outreach'. Most people interpret it as a process that involves going out from a specific organisation or centre to work in other locations with sets of people who typically do not or cannot avail themselves of the services of that centre. While the central connotation of outreach is to physically *go* outside the institution (a staff activity), a number of other meanings have accrued to the word: *activities to make people in different locations or groups aware of what an organisation or centre can offer* (a marketing or recruitment strategy); *provision of learning programmes in informal community locations* (a delivery mechanism); *liaison and contact with other organisations or particular sets of people* (a networking process); *working in particular ways* with people outside the main centre or institution (a method or an approach), as well as any number of other meanings that will be explored below. There can also be a significant difference between an outreach 'project' (which may be short-term and very limited in scope) and outreach work that is integral to an organisation's work. Thus, as observed by Rhodes and Stimson (1994: 9):

> there are many participants involved in the purchasing, provision, consumption and evaluation of outreach services. While each might have differing and competing expectations and desires, it is important that to some extent they speak the same language.

The terms that are used in adult education tend to come in and out of fashion in relation to policy and funding changes. 'Access' is an example of a word that was frequently used in the 1980s and early 1990s to mean inclusion of under-represented groups in adult education and training but the term became increasingly associated with Access (to Higher Education) students and mature students, and has been largely replaced by the term 'participation'. The word outreach has undergone a similar evolution. It was used a lot in the 1970s and 1980s in relation to community-based learning activities but gradually disappeared from the literature in the 1990s, during which some analysts, writing about activities that would have been described as outreach 10-20 years earlier, tended not to use the term at all. Smith (1994: 1-2), for example, did not use it when describing the work of:

educators who engage with local networks and cultures and who build ways of working which connect with local understandings. Their main workplace is not the classroom. Shops, launderettes, streets, pubs, cafés and people's front rooms are the settings.

In the past few years, there has been a tendency for the word 'outreach' to be replaced by other fashionable terms which also imply a reaching out to non-participating sections of the community. Lifelong learning, social inclusion, widening participation – another set of broad terms which can be interpreted in a number of ways – are currently often used to describe activities that would formerly have been labelled outreach. Such terms tend to be used interchangeably depending on which are the buzzwords of the moment or which are the most likely to attract funding. There is an increasing tendency, for example, to conflate the ideas of widening participation and outreach.

I see outreach as a process of widening participation. Widening participation is about access, participation and achievements as a total concept. Any point in that cycle could be out in the community (FE inspector)

Outreach; community development; widening participation; lifelong learning, social inclusion – they're all same sort of bag. This college has assistant principals responsible for lifelong learning, widening participation and community development, but they're all really about the same thing'. (College manager)

If we're bidding for funding we call it [outreach] widening participation (FE outreach worker)

Since restructuring we have had a head of centre for widening participation – a new title with money from the Standards Fund. In last year's bid I was called community and development link worker. In this one, I'm back to network co-ordinator! (FE outreach worker)

A similar process has occurred with other terms used in relation to community-based work: what used to be called community development is now frequently referred to as community regeneration; outreach or community development workers are often referred to as facilitators or animateurs.

Negative connotations

Conversations held during the course of this study suggested that one of the reasons some people have eliminated the word outreach from their vocabulary is because they think it is derogatory and has acquired the connotation of low-level work with less able people:

Some staff regard off-site provision as automatically inferior. (FE outreach worker)

We don't use the word outreach as it is pejorative. We use the word 'link'. (FE college manager)

Some analysts also feel that the use of the word risks sounding patronising or paternalistic since it may imply both that an education centre or institution is the only place where it is possible to learn, or that people need help to remedy learning deficiencies:

The very notion of 'outreach' implies a reaching out from the centre of learning and power and that the institutional centre is the necessary and appropriate starting point. At worst this might reinforce a deficit model of education, in which education-impoverished communities are nourished by learning handouts (Stuart and Thomson, 1995: 10-11)

The term 'outreach' comes from a Christian missionary discourse which suggests that those who do not come to 'worship' or, in adult education language, 'the centre' are in some sense wrong and need 'saving'. Outreach establishes a discourse which makes those adults who do not come into our buildings different from the norm.

There has always been a tension between work with geographically and culturally diverse communities and the physical spaces which adult educators inhabit. The concept of 'outreach work', which is used to describe networking with communities outside our buildings, suggests that there is a right place to learn and that place is in our classrooms and offices. It is not that access to equipment and learning facilities is not important. These resources are vital, but focusing learning in 'a centre' excludes many groups of people who for one reason or another cannot or do not want to come into our buildings. (Clancy and Stuart, 1995: 50)

In some sectors, however, as well as in policy documents, 'outreach' is gradually returning to the educational vocabulary – *We have a project which was called widening participation but is now called outreach* (FE outreach worker) – but, as noted earlier, understandings of the term vary widely.

During the course of this study, a range of different understandings of the term outreach were encountered both in the literature and in conversations with people working in different sectors.

Common understandings of outreach

Outreach is variously understood as:

- **A set of aims**
  To move away from the 'come and get it' approach to adult/further education which clearly does not reach the less confident, the 'disadvantaged', those who don't identify with formal education, the working-class, the vast majority of unemployed and unwaged adults;

    To become more aware of the 'market' for an educational area; to be more directly responsive to the current needs and concerns of people in local communities;

    To identify new groups who have educational needs that are not being met.
  (Johnston, 1986)

- **Activities outside an institution or centre to increase non-user awareness of and participation in education**
  Outreach is frequently used in this sense by practitioners and policy-makers:

    Outreach is a process whereby people who would not normally use adult education are contacted and become involved in attending and eventually in jointly planning and controlling activities, schemes and courses relevant to circumstances and needs. (Ward, 1986)

    It's about developing opportunities for and with people who find difficulty in accessing college opportunities (FE College manager)

    [Outreach is] getting to communities who don't fit in the 'box'. It isn't appropriate to call communities into the box; it is more appropriate to go out to the community and broaden the box. You've got to take it to them instead of asking them to come to you. (FE College manager)

- **A marketing or recruitment strategy**
  Outreach might refer to publicity and enrolment procedures in the community but involve mainstream provision on the main site (voluntary sector worker)

    The word outreach has been used very recently by people in this department – used as a form of marketing, by which I mean marketing and preparation for recruitment which I guess is how most main-site FE people would use the term.

Recruitment is a real issue in continuing education. (HE widening participation officer)

Outreach has been used to describe a marketing exercise when it forms part of a more sophisticated approach to the planning of a course than has conventionally been the case. In this sense, it concentrates attention on the need to target provision at particular groups, and on making contacts with sections of the population who are identified as being under-represented within educational provision.' (Krafchik and Warke, 1988: 3.)

In some cases outreach is also understood as:

- **Publicity events or materials**

  In HE you don't hear the term used on the whole except by people like me (and HEIs have a difficulty with people like me) although they may have dabbled in the community in their continuing education work. I guess if 'outreach' were mentioned at this university, they'd probably be talking about paper or publicity of some kind. Or you'd be referred to schools liaison officers. Open days are also considered to be outreach – because it involves speaking to people outside of a lecture format! (HE widening participation worker)

  One LEA leafleted a local estate and thought that was outreach! (LEA officer)

- **An off-site location: a learning centre or access point away from an institution's main campus or buildings**

  For some formal institutions, outreach means little more than an outside location for learning:

  For me it [outreach] is like a college without walls; the organisation is a hub, a structure but with tentacles all over the place. People think of colleges as a campus or a building but they're not. Some colleges have dozens of centres or points of learning where people begin the journey of learning. (FE inspector)

Some institutional sites are described specifically as outreach, for example the outreach university at Armagh (Queens University).

- **Delivery of community-based provision**

  This is another common understanding of the term, particularly in the formal education sector:

  In its broadest and most commonly used sense outreach can mean FE provision delivered away from the main college site(s)...programmes delivered within the community and away from main campus sites. In this respect, outreach is identified as an essential element in promoting interest and participation in education and training by those who have not traditionally been able or willing to consider it as an option or opportunity. (FEFCW, 1999)

- **Programme and curriculum development**
  Designing new products, new courses, new packaging (REPLAN South West, 1990: 13)

  It's about development of courses in the community (College manager)

  the creation of community-based learning initiatives that allow informed choices for current non participants (Sussex County Council)

- **Targeted provision**
  For many practitioners, outreach has come to mean work targeted at specific groups under-represented in conventional provision:

  Our outreach is targeted provision: the development of particular provision areas either in a specific curriculum area or for a recognised target group (WEA officer)

- **Networking and community liaison**
  For many people, outreach is also a process of community networking:

  I would see it as about a specific activity of contacting people rather than being community-based education as such (HE lecturer)

  A desire to break out of the limitations imposed by college walls, college routines and college regulations; to move closer to people and life in the community; and to establish two-way communication and traffic between college and community. (FEU/REPLAN, 1990: 12-14)

Similarly, some institutions understand it as:

- **Relationships and formal arrangements with other providing organisations**
  Prior to the establishment of Access and Guidance, the University's official outreach policy was well-established but related solely to formal relationships with other educational providers, primarily FE colleges across the region. (Weatherald and Layer, 1998: 63)

- **Support for community groups and organisations**
  Another common meaning is provision of finance, practical help, tutors and premises, as well as responsive learning activities for community groups and organisations:

  Outreach can mean funding outside activities for other organisations that don't necessarily have an interest in the college (College manager)

The outreach worker meeting with women living in a particular estate goes to where they meet, asks direct or indirect questions about what facilities they would like to improve or change their situation, and then brings to them the resources which will make some of that improvement or change possible. These resources may be a tutor or group-worker, some equipment, some transport...and, sometimes, premises (Mace, 1992: 53)

- **A particular approach or style of working**
  Brent and Brent (1992: 4) define outreach in the context of the youth and community service as:

  A style of work (incorporating several different methods) which enables us to make contact and work with young people where they are: in the community....a way of working with and on behalf of young people in the street, in pubs, cafes, schools and community groups.

This kind of approach often involves an 'empowerment' dimension:

- **Community development**
  In community development terms, outreach approaches are an essential part of the process of encouraging individuals and groups to take responsibility for their own learning and to assert control over activities likely to have some chance of influencing change in their local community. (FEU/REPLAN, 1990b: 12-14)

- **A broad incremental process incorporating a number of stages, methods and approaches**
  I see outreach as whatever it takes to engage someone not currently learning in learning. (LEA officer)

  'Outreach' essentially means three things at once: research, consultation and action. The outreach worker goes out with questions and an intention to provide some kind of appropriate answer to them. The guiding principle for both questions and answer is that of consultation. (Mace, 1992: 53)

  Outreach is a process where people who would not normally engage with Higher Education are contacted often in non-institutional settings. Through this contact a dialogue is initiated with a view to identifying the learning needs of the people contacted, their interest in and potential for HE and exactly what HE is able to offer them immediately and in the longer-term. The outreach process can involve: the identification of specific target groups who are under-represented in HE or face particular barriers in engaging in HE; active collaboration with outside partners; initial negotiation of the curriculum. A next stage in the outreach negotiation process might often be a short 'taster' course which would usually be held on familiar territory for the learners. (working definition adopted by the Wessex Solent Partnership for Widening Participation, 2000)

Thus outreach has been defined variously as off-site provision; as a method of learning delivery; as support for the community; as a networking process; as targeted provision; as curriculum development; as marketing; as a way or style of working; as a set of particular aims or as a broad and multifaceted process involving numerous activities and stages. People talking or writing about outreach may have some or all of these meanings in mind although the locational emphasis tends to be paramount. The widespread tendency to define outreach as any activities conducted off-site has its limitations. If outreach is only understood as learning activities or programmes delivered outside institutions in order to enable a wider mix of people to access them, does this mean that any ICT-based learning that takes place outside dedicated learning environments should be labelled 'outreach'? And should HE provision delivered in further education colleges also be described as 'outreach' even though it might be delivered in the formal setting of a college's main site, whereas the college's own outreach provision might be provided in satellite centres, community locations or employers' premises?

The common interpretation of outreach as off-site activity also puts the focus on provision and neglects the dimension of 'process', which many people believe is crucial to the whole concept of outreach.

In many education institutions there is a tendency to conflate outreach and marketing, with managers seeing outreach purely as a way of facilitating supply of education provision and services and stimulating demand through: '"selling" the idea and relevance of education through a variety of publicity media or institutional contacts' (Johnston, 1992: 72). Johnston warns that this approach can limit student choice, unlike a more responsive demand-led strategy.

> *Current economic pressures and existing budgetary constraints and targets often make it very difficult to embark on any long-term marketing strategy that goes beyond developing a token dialogue with non-traditional student groups. The result can often be that the unwaged adult is allocated a passive role in making a purely reactive choice from a limited 'menu' of educational possibilities.*
>
> *In contrast, an outreach approach may be less concerned with finding a market for its potential educational provision (supply/institution-led) than making education responsive to the prevailing concerns and interests of those in the local community (demand-led). It tries to move away from ideas of educational consumerism and to view the educational process as much more of a dialogue. In fact, it aims to go beyond immediately articulated wants to discover latent needs over a longer period of time. This clearly involves a process of negotiation.*
> (Johnston, 1992: 71-72)

Wood (1999) also makes a distinction between outreach as a marketing tool to sell a product or as a market research tool to ensure 'the right product is offered at the right time and the right price', and outreach as a way of working with people to generate learning programmes that meet their own agenda. The first she classifies as a supermarket or top-down model in which specific products are on offer to potential customers (for example, a set course in a specific location at a set cost, the outreach element being publicity or taster sessions). The second she classifies as a bottom-up or community model which involves finding out about the targeted community or area; making initial contacts and engaging with local people as a route to individual and group development.

Outreach is also commonly understood as a process of reaching and engaging with people who cannot, or do not want to, use conventionally provided services. In this sense it can apply to a wide range of activities in a wide range of sectors. Organisations which realise that their established structures are not meeting the needs of certain groups or that there are segments of the population who cannot, or choose not to, use them, have to find ways of reaching these groups outside their traditional structures. Obvious examples are religious sects sending out proselytisers or missionaries; financial institutions which have initiated postal or computer banking services; commercial concerns which sell through the Internet; cultural organisations (theatres, opera companies, art galleries) which go 'on tour' in different parts of the country.

Reasons for doing outreach

As this suggests, the reasons for doing outreach usually determine understandings of it. In an education context, these may be: to identify new groups who have not been reached and who may have learning needs that are not being met; to recruit people to existing provision by raising their awareness of opportunities; to increase the provider's understanding of local community needs and concerns; to take services to people who are unable to access provision because of family responsibilities or difficulties with costs and transport; to develop new methods of educational delivery. It may also be undertaken because there are some groups of people for whom outreach services are particularly appropriate (eg people in residential or day centres); because the institution wants or is required to increase its numbers of students, or because there is funding attached to attracting particular groups of people such as those from specific postcode areas. Some rather cynically suggest that in certain institutions there is little interest in outreach beyond the funding made available for it: 'I don't think the old universities want to widen participation to different groups, especially if they're popular institutions' (University lecturer).

Thus the reasons for engaging in outreach may be either altruistic or opportunistic, or, as often happens, a combination of the two:

Within this college there are both attitudes. Outreach equals recruitment and money (which is the view of managers) and outreach equals helping people (which is the view of outreach workers) (FE outreach worker)

Thus outreach may mean different things in different contexts and the definitions used can vary according to the occupational position and viewpoint of the person you are talking to:

People will see it differently as an organisational concept, an educational concept or a funding concept. If you talk to people involved in accreditation and funding you'll be told something different from an inspector! (FEFC inspector)

In short, the word 'outreach' has multiple and sometimes competing meanings. As Rhodes and Stimson (1994: 9) assert:

The word conflates a myriad of meanings, practices and promises...Different purchasers and providers from different...sectors understand the fundamental aims, objectives and practices of 'outreach' very differently. Whether one decides to celebrate or to criticise 'outreach' depends largely on whose outreach we are talking about and what exactly we expect it to achieve. If purchasers are to purchase outreach effectively, and if providers are to provide it efficiently, there needs to be mutual understanding of the basic models and elements of outreach work.

This raises the question of whether the term 'outreach' is now too imprecise to be useful. Some believe that it has become an outdated concept that has been overtaken by developments such as distance learning, ICT-based learning and flexible learning packages that enable learning to take place in a variety of different modes and environments (Clancy and Stuart, 1995). Nevertheless, the word is currently re-emerging in policy papers and the adult educational vocabulary, albeit often with a particular set of associations.

Outreach and disadvantaged communities

In the discourses of current policy and funding documents, two notions continually recur – the notion of 'community' and the notion of 'disadvantage'. Both of these have become inextricably bound up with the concept of outreach and both, like the word 'outreach' itself, need deconstructing.

Like 'outreach', the term 'community' has acquired multiple meanings and connotations. There are a number of common understandings of the term, some examples of which are given below:

A distinctive name, a recognisable dialect, and the adoption of commonly agreed territorial boundaries are the three necessary conditions which, if met, grant to a collection of individuals and buildings the term 'community'. (Brookfield, 1983: 65)

A community is a specific group of people actually living in a defined geographical area who share a common culture and exhibit some awareness of their identity as a group. (Rhodes and Stimpson, 1994: 9)

Community can be defined in three ways: the geographical community in which you live; the community to which you belong by nature of your race, gender etc., and the community which you join either through choice e.g. a political party, or one to which you are assigned, e.g. refugee. (Dinsdale, 1999: 2)

As is often noted, however, the term 'community' has acquired connotations beyond its literal meaning as people living in a defined location, or groups with shared characteristics or interests. It has been described as a 'warm' word (Smith, 1994); one that denotes both 'a fact and a value' (Fremeaux, 2000), and one which, according to Brookfield (1983: 60-61):

has the power to inspire a reverential suspension of critical judgement in the minds of adult educators, social workers and those within the caring and health professions. It is as if in invoking this term adult educators thereby imbue their practice with a humanistic concern and an almost self-righteous compassion which pre-empts any considered analysis of its central features…. 'Community'… can be attached to almost any activity in an attempt to imbue such work with a sense of compassion and concern.

Brookfield (p. 61) warns against 'the semantic and conceptual trap' of attaching the label 'community' to any adult education practice which is felt to be desirable, since this imbues it with prescriptive as well as descriptive associations: 'To assert that one is practising "community" adult education is to declare that one is doing something which is innately desirable as well as to describe practice.'

It is difficult to find a recent social or educational policy document which does not repeatedly refer to community in this sense. The current overuse of the term has been captured in a recent cartoon in a national newspaper. This shows one man glaring at another with the caption: 'if you mention the word community again I'll kill you!'. As Martin (1992: 29) has observed, the connotations of the word have now become more important than its literal meanings: *The key point is that 'community' is primarily an evaluative, and only secondarily a descriptive, concept.*

Although the locational emphasis remains strong and adult education providers still commonly use place as a way of identifying a community, some analysts now question whether location *per se* defines a community. It is

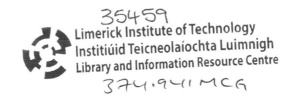

argued that the mere fact of residing in a particular area no longer leads to the formation of a homogeneous community as social and economic changes together with developments in communications have resulted in the loss of shared experience and a shared perspective on the world:

> *In our world of 'virtual connection', where proximity ceases to be determinant of contact, the very question of what constitutes a 'community' is an open one.* (OECD, 1999: 20)

Moreover, as outreach workers routinely find, a huge diversity of cultures, attitudes and interests can co-exist within a very small geographical area:

> *The mere fact of neighbourhood habitation carries within it no inherent predisposition towards community. An area of two or three square miles in a city may contain an astonishingly diverse collection of groups, the membership and focus of which will shift over time.* (Brookfield, 1983: 65)

> *Most people did not relate to the Estate as a whole, but to individual blocks or groups of blocks of flats, and some to the side streets at the periphery. It also has communities of interest, e.g. the tenants' groups, the parents' groups associated with particular schools and communities defined by age, e.g. the teenagers who gathered on the walkways and at the chip shop, and the elderly people who had lived in Walworth for many years....All these, and other, communities exist side by side, overlapping to some degree.* (Nicholls and Murray, 1981: 58)

> *From the outside it is difficult to tell where one community area starts and the other ends. Boundaries are sometimes framed by subtle, internal, social distinctions not connected with architectural planning* (Trotman and Pudner, 1998: 48-49)

> *We've had people say: 'We're not going there, we're not going into a class with that lot'. You talk to the two different communities, and one lot say, 'they're a bit snobby', and the other lot say 'they're a bit rough there', and there is only half a mile separating them.* (quoted in Wood, 2000)

Community and disadvantage

In the last part of the twentieth century, the term 'community' acquired additional connotations. Fremeux (2000: 49-50) analyses how economic and social changes, together with 'massive' programmes of public housing, transport and urban renewal, disrupted spatial communities, as a result of which the notion of community increasingly took on a new set of meanings connected with social deprivation and 'system dysfunction':

community became and seemingly persistently, the answer to the predicament of the poor and underprivileged. Since the late 1960s, policy makers have quite consistently used the term to refer to the socially excluded.

She observes that community used in this sense is a strong theme of New Labour policy. Alongside this meaning, however, also developed the idea of community in terms of collective or grassroots action. The active involvement of people in the design and implementation of urban renewal programmes was proposed in the 1969 Skeffington Report (Ministry of Housing and Local Government, 1969) and led to the creation of Community Development Projects which, according to Fremeaux, completely contradicted the idea of social dysfunction. She relates how, in the 1980s, the two opposing views and discourses came into direct collision: those of central government as outlined above, and those of left-wing authorities (such as the Greater London Council) which were developing radical new programmes and supporting communities based on gender, race and other identities. It was an unequal battle: resources for local authorities were sharply reduced, with the result that different community groups became locked in competition for financial support, each having to demonstrate its greater need:

groups not only became highly dependent on these programmes but also got into dire competition for scarce resources. This resulted in exacerbation of boundaries between communities of difference. Moreover the late 1980s saw an acceleration of the process through which attributions of government resources were made according to pre set performance criteria rather than need. (Fremeaux, 2000: 50)

According to Fremeaux, this history has left the word 'community' with several associations that are now simultaneously understood by the term:

It refers to socially deprived areas (locally defined); it is a positive and normative entity featured by inclusiveness and solidarity, and its mention triggers a series of practical methods to be put into practice. Thus consultation, participation, local involvement, partnerships, capacity building, training opportunities, empowering practices have become the golden path to urban renewal and every project implemented within such a framework is conceptualised following those principles. (Fremeaux, 2000: 51)

These dimensions of meaning are all implicit in the use of the term in policy initiatives relating to social inclusion, lifelong learning and widening participation, and it is in relation to them that current outreach initiatives should be seen.

CHAPTER TWO

Current practice

Methods and models

It is perhaps in sectors such as health, youth and community work that one finds the clearest expositions of outreach methods. Brent and Brent (1992), for example, distinguish between four different methods used in youth work, each of which has an equivalent in adult education:

- *Satellite work* (the opening up and staffing of a satellite office, club or group in an area that is not otherwise serviced);
- *Peripatetic work* (workers using their skills in various existing youth work arenas as required) ;
- *Community work* (relationships with community groups and individuals in order to raise awareness and progress work) ;
- *Street work* (working with and building relationships with the target groups wherever they are).

In their HIV-related outreach work, Rhodes and Stimpson (1994) differentiate between:

- *Detached outreach* which takes place outside of agency or organisational settings, for example in streets, pubs, cafés, bars and station concourses;
- *Peripatetic outreach* which focuses on organisations rather than individuals (work in hostels, youth clubs, schools and prisons); and
- *Domiciliary outreach* which involves visiting the homes of target populations.

Again, these have their equivalents in adult education practice with many outreach workers using a combination of these approaches. Rhodes and Stimpson (1994) also distinguish two main types of outreach strategy – *individual outreach* which targets individuals on a one-to-one basis in order to change behaviour and bring about individual or self-empowerment, and *community outreach* which targets groups or communities with the aim of achieving community change and empowerment. Both of these models can be found in current education practice. For example, a handbook for lifelong learning in Wales (Francis, 1999) includes a range of outreach models used in working with both groups and individuals. These include:
- mobile services including careers units and IT

- provision in community locations (sometimes used as stepping stone into mainstream)
- dedicated outreach schemes and venues (such as the Valleys Initiative for Adult Education, the Community University; an Outreach College)
- targeted outreach (such as work with carers and parents of young children)
- distance learning models and IT learning networks for people in remote locations (for example, Llandrillo Learning Network which incorporates Cyberskills: the extension of learning opportunities to people in communities and workplaces through electronic communication and partnership with organisations and employers)
- capacity-building training for grassroots workers

Partnerships and networking are strong features of all these models. The Valleys' Initiative for Adult Education, for example, is a network model aimed at supporting cross-sectoral networking amongst organisations and individuals working in lifelong learning with the overall aim of community regeneration and transformation.

In England, the demonstration outreach projects involved in a DfEE-funded initiative (Watson and Tyers, 1998) involved a similar range of models, notably:

- taking information and advice on existing opportunities into the community
- provision of courses in outreach locations as a stepping stone to mainstream provision
- training of local volunteers as learning champions
- activities tailored to the needs of specific targeted groups
- initiatives involving ICT.

According to Watson and Tyers, three main models emerged:

- Delivering services on an outreach model which typically involved professionals from mainstream education or guidance providers taking their services out onto estates.
- Using volunteer residents on estates as 'ambassadors' for learning.
- Training workers with an existing role on the estate as 'front-line' education and guidance workers.

Another effective approach used in the demonstration projects was to use current learners and volunteers as conduits to their friends, neighbours and family, and to use local people to promote activities A project in Hackney used local workers, recruited from the community, to assist in the promotion and running of activities; in Norwich, children were given invitations to 'family workshops' to pass on to their parents.

An increasingly popular outreach strategy is to use mobile services to reach sections of the population living in spread-out estates or urban and rural areas that are poorly supplied, if at all, with educational and guidance services. Many of these carry publicity materials, and have a crèche and kitchen area. A number also carry computers for IT training.

These models typify the kind of outreach approaches currently being employed in different education sectors, some examples of which will be outlined below.

Diversity of practice

The extent to which education and training providers currently engage in outreach (in all the senses outlined in the previous chapter) varies widely. Organisations and institutions inevitably differ in their commitment to and ability to conduct locally-based or -directed activities. Some do very little; others a great deal. Those which cater mainly for adults such as the Workers' Educational Association (WEA) and the adult residential colleges routinely undertake various forms of outreach activities. Northern College, for example, which was established to respond to the learning interests and needs of socially, economically and educationally disadvantaged groups, has outreach as a central organising concept. Tutor organisers visit and work with community groups in different areas and negotiate bespoke courses based on identified learning interests and requirements. Many local education authorities use a range of community venues for delivering short courses for adults but other kinds of outreach activities were reduced after the introduction of the Schedule 2/non-Schedule 2 funding divide in the wake of the 1992 Further and Higher Education Act. Further education institutions, which have a more varied clientele and wider mission, differ greatly in their practices and the study found a range of views regarding the sector's involvement with local communities.

Kennedy (1997) saw further education as a major vehicle for widening participation and meeting local needs, and Green and Lucas (1999: 230) assert that colleges, despite their experience of incorporation, are:

> *still embedded in local communities and historically have had good links with sectors of the community which are now seen as potential sites for the dispersed learning opportunities envisioned in the 'learning society'. They have close connections with employers, professional bodies and community associations, as well as 'outreach' operations which extend their activities into housing estates.*

A number of informants to this study, however (including further education staff and managers), were not convinced of the sector's capacity or preparedness to engage with their local communities:

FE per se *doesn't have a tradition of going onto an estate and putting on stuff for a target group. There's still a wariness in FE about going onto the estates. My college isn't quite sure what is meant by community development. It doesn't really know what it wants to develop and what it wants to do. We do very little grassroots work. All outside work is very formalised and partnered. The college feels safer in partnership; not taking any risks. We're really doing widening participation and lifelong learning from an FEFC perspective which is 'bums on seats' or more students for the same money.* (FE manager)

If you asked colleges whether they work in the community they'll say ' of course!' But they don't! They're not used to working in the community; they may have outreach workers but it's really taking the college out into the community not listening to the community. That's not real outreach. They think along the lines of numbers and won't do anything which won't have any visible short-term or long- term (by which they mean six months) outcomes. One college here is locked into a very deprived area and they say they do 'outreach' but it isn't really that: they take a recruitment desk out of college and plonk it in the community somewhere. (Former FE manager)

They're {the college} dead scared of the voluntary sector because they can't do this widening participation thing! (FE outreach worker)

Getting colleges to take this kind of thing seriously rather than a bolt-on is very difficult. (LEA outreach worker)

Some higher education informants involved in widening participation initiatives were equally sceptical about that sector's ability to conduct outreach, as the following comments from four of them demonstrate:

Universities don't have a history of going out and learning about people's lived experience despite their being research institutions. So much of widening participation is focused on the 14-18 group and not on the next cohort – the 19-30 who have missed out. There doesn't even seem to be any concern about the drop in number of mature students.

Though there is a genuine belief in widening participation and that we should be doing it, they'd really rather get high paying overseas students than work in the community. There's still a feeling that they're not our sort of people. Although some universities have had to attract local communities.

The university finds the notion of taking things off campus extremely challenging. Outreach is still seen as a high risk strategy. Widening participation and lifelong learning are seen as dumbing down; threatening the whole university.

The term outreach is used here but I haven't been able to nail it down. In terms of lifelong learning and widening participation, outreach is seen as making a contribution but God alone knows what and how!

In both sectors, however, there is growing recognition of the need to extend opportunities beyond mainstream provision on main campuses in response to policy and funding developments such as funding for partnerships, postcode weightings and money for widening participation initiatives.

Further education

In further education, strategic funding for growth in 1999-2000 included widening participation as one of the priorities. In addition, non-Schedule 2 funding was allocated on a wider basis, with institutions invited to set up pilots to encourage wider participation and social inclusion. These developments, together with new initiatives such as UfI, are encouraging colleges to engage or re-engage in outreach activities:

In the early days of incorporation there was a drop as we geared ourselves to what FEFC wanted. The college mission has changed. Now we're looking to do more outreach work prior to UfI. (College manager)

At last the college is making an effort to get out and talk to people. (Outreach worker)

Colleges ditched it [outreach] about 8 years ago; now some are going back as though nothing has happened. (LEA worker)

In Wales, where postcode-weighted funding was introduced several years ago, colleges have been active in making connections with their local communities. According to one study this has largely been achieved by delivering outreach provision in a range of local venues (Francis, 1999). Analysis of student data for 1997-98 (FEFCW, 1999) showed that outreach work of this kind has expanded, with a variety of approaches used, ranging from opening entire campuses in community locations, to delivering programmes on a small local scale, sometimes through third parties. However, the study found that although some institutions have been trying to respond to expressed community needs, most outreach involves delivery of conventional provision in off-site centres. Enrolments at such sites represented 27 per cent of all enrolments in FE institutions, with the courses offered broadly similar to those on main sites (art, design and the performing arts; caring and health; computing; secretarial and office technology; adult basic education, English for speakers of other languages, Welsh for adults and other general education). Just over 15 per cent of the total number of outreach sites were located in the most deprived wards in Wales, with provision offered directly by an FE institution or delivered on a third-party basis by a local authority in venues such as community centres, religious centres and schools. However, the range of programmes on offer in the most deprived areas was narrower than for outreach provision in general and the study concluded that despite evidence of a growing use of local venues and penetration into communities where participation in post-school education is low, there remain a number of areas where learning opportunities are not yet provided.

The satellite centre model and use of informed community venues are probably the most common outreach strategies for further education in England, and there are countless examples. Park Lane College in Leeds and Knowsley Community College deliver programmes in a very large number of community-based venues. Some institutions such as Selby College and Farnborough College use local pubs as outreach centres to persuade people to return to learning. Some sixth-form colleges are also engaging in more community-focused work. Woking 6th Form College, for example, has a community liaison section.

The following examples illustrate the kind of outreach approaches that are currently being employed in colleges:

Knowsley Community College is situated in an area of high unemployment with a younger than average population and a large number of single parent families. The Borough Council is the biggest local employer, followed by the college and Fords.

The college's widening participation funding factor is the highest outside London and in its FEFC report in 1997-98 the college was described as an excellent exemplar for widening participation.

The college has a community participation unit (CPU) which has 30 full-time and 42 part-time teaching staff and nine administrative staff. There are three senior outreach co-ordinators and one outreach co-ordinator working under the leadership of a development manager, as well as two sessional workers who work in specific local areas. There are also two dedicated guidance workers attached to Student Services who operate outside the college.

Most CPU courses are delivered on an outreach basis at local 'linc' centres (Learning in Neighbourhood Centres): 'We don't use the word outreach as it is pejorative.' There are 123 of these, 60 per cent of which are primary schools. Others are located in youth clubs, libraries, community centres, blocks of flats and other community venues: 'Wherever you live in Knowsley there is a college centre within 200-300 yards of your home.'

Each centre has a designated person who is paid a small sum in return for taking responsibility for that centre. The system is formula-funded: every time a student attends, this generates a certain sum for the centre (eg 55p for a part-time student; 85p for an ABE student and £1.11 for a full-time student). In addition there is an achievement payment 'bonus' of £5 to the centre for every student that attains a particular outcome. This encourages the centres to work with the College in helping students to achieve.

Resources are targeted at the most disadvantaged areas of the borough and at specific groups such as ex-offenders, drug users, disaffected youth and people using family centres.

The curriculum is demand-led and negotiated with groups and individuals. The Unit's policy is to make a rapid response to any demands identified (for example, within less than a week of their arrival, a tailor-made programme comprising English, computing and crafts was set up for Kosovan refugees). Programmes are modularised and tuition is free (although there is some payment for accreditation with concessions offered to those who are unemployed).

The role of outreach workers is to engage local people in conversation about education and training. The current team are all women and, in accordance with unit policy, all former students who act as role models. They contact people at school gates, mother and toddler groups, parent evenings, Bingo halls, clubs and community and town centres. There is also a college trailer which visits town centres on a regular basis (every day during Adult Learners' Week). The workers also liaise with centre co-ordinators, assisting with enrolments and supporting tutors, and build relationships with other local providers.

Many of the people contacted by the Unit, especially those in their 30s, want to obtain some qualifications. Accordingly, all pre-vocational courses have been OCN accredited although the college has now been contracted to do Non-Schedule 2 pilots with 200 students, and has also obtained funding to work with disengaged youth and long-term unemployed. Outreach techniques will be used in recruiting these

Student progression is encouraged in a number of ways. Part of the lifelong learning strategy is to build links between CPU and other college sections. Some CPU courses have therefore been designed in collaboration with mainstream vocational areas such as motor vehicle maintenance, catering. IT, creative studies, and music. To facilitate progression, staff bring students into the college at appropriate times so that they can become familiar with the premises, staff and facilities. Outreach students are treated like mainstream college students (for example, they all receive student diaries) which makes them feel part of the college and encourages continuation of learning. Learning achievements are celebrated at public ceremonies every year in town centres.

Evaluation and outcomes

Because outreach is perceived as a mainstream activity, it is subject to the same quality procedures as all college work and there is a process of constant monitoring in the form of observation of classes, staff appraisals, programme review, team meetings, student satisfaction surveys and collection of achievement and retention figures. There are also specific Performance Indicators, both core and developing, for outreach work. These include indicators for enrolments, retention and progression (with targets for each subject offered). An annual action plan and review identifies action points for the following year, and there is continuous monitoring for cost-effectiveness.

Three years ago, a cost-benefit analysis revealed that in purely financial terms the outreach activities make a loss; however, the work is seen as an important investment in the college's future. Since 1993, student numbers through the CPU have risen from 323 to 4,000 and there is a 75 per cent retention rate. Destination data is collected from all students. This shows that many former students have become classroom assistants (after attending classroom assistant courses), volunteers and adult tutors. In 1999, 420 computer literacy students found employment. One example of success is an ex-Access student who has become chief librarian in the local area.

There is also evidence of progression into mainstream college courses. In 1999, 538 CPU students entered the college and 88 per cent of young adults on the 'Roll over Beethoven' music course moved into certificated FE courses. Of 174 students who took only CPU courses in 1998-99, 59 went into the main college, 102 into other CPU courses at outreach venues, and 13 into both: 'Outreach is seen as a gateway.' However, a member of staff warned that: 'it is not always appropriate to expect progression with all of our outreach students. There's a time to push and a time to leave well alone. You have to be sensitive to that.' She mentioned outcomes that are less tangible but potentially more important than progression into mainstream, notably the knock-on impact parental learning is having on the motivation of local school children:

A lot of local schools say that their Ofsted reports were much better than expected. There are positive spin-offs from parents learning – it's cool to be in school. In a place like this where there are appalling GCSE rates, we need as many positive role models as possible. If you've got mum, auntie, brother or sister in long-term education and training, the impact is incalculable. If we didn't believe that we would have chopped it years ago because if you only take progression into account you'd obviously be making a loss.

A number of colleges employ an outreach approach which involves group rather than area targeting. A good example of this is Oaklands College in St Albans.

Oaklands College is a large general further education college with campuses in mid and south Hertfordshire, in Borehamwood, St Albans and Welwyn Garden City. The College is the product of the merger of three colleges (including an agricultural college) in 1992. It currently belongs to the Hertfordshire Lifelong Learning Partnership which is co-ordinated through the LEA and has worked with the other three Hertfordshire colleges as part of an FEFC Widening Participation project to map and audit participation ward by ward.

The College has no formal policy on outreach work although it is a clear priority in its strategic objectives: 'We have prioritised inclusive learning as the framework within which we are widening and increasing participation. This is the key driving force behind what we do and how we do it.'

The College has a diverse range of community activity which can be segmented into:

- franchise work
- non-vocational work
- work with people with learning difficulties and/or disabilities
- community initiatives.

Franchise work comprises 5 per cent of the College's activity and is focused on community and voluntary organisations within its catchment. In addition there is a significant open and distance learning scheme.

A range of leisure programmes are run both on College premises and in community venues. They are attended by 5,000 students catering for a wide range of interests.

The College has a strong tradition of working with people with learning difficulties and/or disabilities. It was recently awarded the Beacon Award for its work with students with profound and complex learning difficulties and challenging behaviour. The College operates contracts through the Local Education Authority and the Horizon Trust. It also runs a range of provision in day centres, including IT provision with MIND in Hatfield.

A range of other work takes place under the umbrella of community initiatives. The college has two dedicated outreach workers, one recruited from the Bosnian community and working both with that community and with Kosovan refugees. The other is working with the Asian community in St Albans, particularly with the Bangladeshi community. Guidance workers also carry out home visits in the Asian community. The College also conducts outreach activities with travellers, family literacy groups, young mothers identified at risk, ex-offenders, disaffected young people and excluded 14-16-year-olds. In working with these groups there is extensive collaboration with other agencies such as social services, employment services, Hertfordshire TEC, the LEA and the probation service.

The College has a community liaison committee to which all formally constituted community organisations in its catchment area are invited. The purpose of the group is to provide a forum for identifying learning needs and services in the community that the College can supply. Recent examples of work include the provision of craft and ESOL training for Asian women, IT training for Bosnian refugees and support for a research project for an Afro-Caribbean group. Use of the College's facilities by community groups is encouraged for meetings and celebrations and as an administrative base.

The College is also involved in a number of partnerships supporting community-based activities. It is a member of the board of Worknet, which offers a range of services within the Borehamwood community, and a partner and board member in the development of the Hatfield Foyer, working with a housing association and a district council to meet the needs of young people who require stable housing arrangements as a platform for personal and employment development. In partnership with West Hertfordshire College and the Hertfordshire TEC, it has developed an outreach centre at Leavesden Studio to provide the training to support the development of the film industry in Hertfordshire. It has also contributed to the funding of The Base, a community youth centre, together with St Albans City and District Council and the Health Authority. In addition, the College provides a range of services on employers' premises and is continuing to work to develop these, supported by structural changes within the college. Ufl will contribute to the further development of this work.

According to a college manager:

The range of outreach work we are involved with is diverse and as a result is not easy to categorise. Similarly the funding of the work relies on a range of sources associated with the partners involved. There is still much to do. We need to formalise our work particularly with the voluntary sector, including recognising that some agencies are better at meeting the needs of some groups than the College, while ensuring a network of 'joined up' suppliers. Reaching out to groups who continue to prove difficult to connect with is also a priority. These include older males, the long-term unemployed and – a perennial problem in an area of high employment – people with limited basic skills who are in employment. There aren't many groups we haven't reached. The issue is what more can we do and how do we get more people involved? We already have wide contacts and referrals from a wide range of agencies. The issue is really the extent: what more work can we do with travellers, for example, or people with basic education or special needs, and what can we do better than we are doing?

Some college outreach work is organised around specific areas of the curriculum, such as adult basic education and English for speakers of other languages (ESOL). A good example of this is the ESOL Network Project based at the College of North East London.

The College of North East London has over 20,000 students, many of them unemployed and over 19. It has about six outreach staff and conducts outreach activities at Broadwater Farm and Northumberland Park Estate where courses are provided in areas such as ESOL, IT and basic skills in local sites, with opportunities for progression into mainstream. These courses are FEFC-funded. There is also an SRB-funded Adult Basic Education network, a worker involved in youth training across the borough and single outreach projects such as tele-working for lone parents.

The ESOL Network Project was proposed by a manager of the college and set up in 1996 in partnership with Tottenham Task Force and North London TEC. The project is based in Haringey and Enfield where there are high proportions of immigrants and where the need for training in English language skills is expanding. Haringey has a large number of asylum seekers and refugees including Turkish Kurds, Cypriots, Somalis, East Europeans and, recently, Kosovans. In 1996-97, 50 per cent of those without English were not involved in ESOL provision and those with least English were least likely to enrol, particularly women with childcare responsibilities. Enfield has a higher proportion of established immigrants, particularly Asian communities (Bangladeshi) and those least likely to seek help with English are women and elderly people.

The project (which is not specifically described as an outreach project) was initiated in recognition of the expanding need for ESOL, the need to train members of the different ethnic communities in teaching ESOL and awareness of need for higher standards in this kind of provision. The overall aim was to enhance the quality of ESOL activity in a Single Regeneration Budget (SRB) area.

The Network has a full-time co-ordinator on secondment from the Department of Continuing Education. She delivers training, organises the ESOL Network which was established in the first year of the project, and assists with advice on suitable accreditation schemes, getting centres approved to run schemes, obtaining resources and staff appointments.

Funding

The project has been funded through the TEC with SRB funding on a capacity-building theme. The college's contribution is in kind: accommodation for the co-ordinator and management of the financial arrangements. At the time of writing continuation funding was uncertain. The project was in its third year of SRB funding and had a verbal agreement for a further two years, but there was some doubt about the future of the TEC in the light of the Learning and Skills Council proposals.

Process and activities

The co-ordinator started her work within a defined geographical area. She did not target particular communities but looked specifically for those involved in ESOL. Although she already knew a number of community groups, it took at least three months of contacts and visiting to get the project up and running:

> *This kind of work takes an awful lot of time. It could have taken me a whole week just contacting one or two organisations as some {TEC and LEA} directories are very out of date. The whole of the first year which I spent visiting and explaining – was an uphill struggle making contact. The contacts and recruitment I did in the first year didn't really get the right people. We were getting people who already knew the networks and appreciated what I was doing and were able to get release. Since then it has generated its own contacts and referrals. We've been over-subscribed and reaching the right people in the smaller community groups. Once trust was gained, the bush telegraph took over and there was a real snowball.*

The groups contacted are offered accredited training in teaching ESOL. The initial teacher training is free and based in the college although there is a teaching placement in different locations. The training leads to a C&G certificate in basic skills (which has an ESOL component) or Open College Network accreditation. Guidance is given at the end of the training and each student develops an action plan. There are possibilities for progression into mainstream and students receive information on other college programmes such as the Cert.Ed. For other higher-level qualifications such as CELTA (Certificate of English Language Teaching for Adults) or the higher C&G certificate, students are referred to other institutions.

Many students are from refugee communities. Some already have a background in teaching and hold qualifications; some are people who have already been teaching ESOL and some are volunteers who are teaching but lack training and qualifications.

The project is 'hooked into the raising standards agenda' with the aim of training tutors to do ESOL, supporting them in what they're doing and raising the standard of what they're doing. The co-ordinator is required to achieve negotiated targets on jobs, qualifications and number of groups supported. The targets are negotiated between the college and the TEC. Although there were initial difficulties in meeting the job outcomes because of the scarcity of full-time jobs in ESOL, more realistic targets were eventually negotiated.

Outcomes

To date, the project has proved its value in raising the standards of ESOL teaching. Some students have acquired part-time and full-time jobs after doing the training and others have gone into higher-level training. Of the 29 trainees who completed City and Guilds 9281 training or Open College TESOL modules in 1998-99, 13 went on to further training, 11 (previously not employed) are now employed in teaching ESOL and five have continued teaching ESOL.

The project is also benefiting the college:

- by increasing recruitment (the network generates additional demand for ESOL training provision, leading to more community based provision for which the college provides qualified tutors)
- by improving public relations (it has led to more favourable perceptions of the college in the community and among voluntary sector organisations)
- by leading to an increase in parent groups requiring tutors for school-based provision
- by raising staff awareness of community needs and encouraging some to work in the community
- by making the college's ESOL staff more representative of the communities they serve (some of the ESOL students are now working for the college).

In addition to these outcomes the project has established an ESOL Network which belongs to members, not to the college – something that is considered very important. Meetings are hosted by members in different venues and held once a term. At first these tended to attract mostly professional and training groups. Now they are attended by about 20 to 25 people, many of whom come from community groups.

The Network has produced several important resources. It has produced a directory of ESOL provision and is developing a quality assurance document; it has compiled a set of realistic and achievable guidelines for good practice in ESOL which have been comprehensively reviewed in the light of members' feedback; and it has also put together a pack for New Deal advisers, TEC and ESOL providers etc., to enable initial assessments of people with ESOL needs. These have been disseminated to the TEC and Employment Services and distributed through the Network.

According to the co-ordinator a critical success factor in all this work has been the support of a senior college manager.

The establishment of new funding sources has enabled some colleges to engage in outreach activities in order to contribute to the process of building community capacity.

With the support of Adult and Community Learning Fund, **South Trafford College** has been working with tenants on an estate to help them manage the transfer of council housing to Housing Association tenure, which involves them in the running of estates: 'For tenants this is a sudden change from being totally ignored to having their opinions asked.'

The aims of the project have been to support tenants through the transfer process, to offer underpinning basic skills training, and to reach people and meet their learning needs on their own terms. To meet these aims the College has been working in partnership with tenants' associations, community organisations (a credit union, church, community groups, a women's group), a local school, the Housing Department and Housing Association, the Credit Union, the Youth Service and Trafford Council.

Activities up to April 2000 included community training, book-keeping, a garden and tool hire club, skills training, training volunteers to support an after-school facility, computer training and a community video project (which the Housing Association has decided to use as a promotional tool). There has also been a residential programme involving three weekends, set up with Fircroft College.

Although divisions and conflicts between different groups of tenants have limited full take-up of the project (the estate has three distinct parts and cultures), the overall impact nevertheless appears to have been significant. A number of individuals have acquired confidence in using IT and video and some have gained OCN accreditation. The project is now training people to run their own IT training. In addition, the community is involved in new working relationships and has acquired a more positive perception of different agencies.

Overall, the project has made people aware of new opportunities and raised expectations. It has also helped to heal some of the mutual antagonism between groups (through mutual involvement in residential work and a health day).

The project has also had a positive impact on the College: new partnerships have been formed with the new housing association, with two schools and the local library service in Trafford). It now has new community bases in which to deliver education and training, and staff have acquired new skills through the delivery and management of the programme.

The factors which have contributed to these outcomes are identified as:

- previous College outreach activity on the estate
- the use of volunteers: 'we were tapping into people's passionate commitment and enthusiasm'
- the flexibility of ACLF funding: 'ACLF funding made things happen in contrast to other funding with all their paperwork and bureaucracy. We couldn't have done it within funding constraints of the College.' (Information from the presentation by Carl Morrison, South Trafford College, to the NIACE Conference *Quality and Equality*, 30–31 March 2000)

Higher education

The higher education sector has also been increasing its work in the community in response to recent policy thrusts although, according to McNair (1999: 58-59), there are wide differences between institutions in the extent and quality of such work:

> while most universities have traditionally recognised this work, its level and quality have been very variable, and it appears to be in decline as a result of other pressures on institutions and their staff. Where institutions have been maintaining or strengthening community links, they are much more likely to be with employers, around economic objectives, than with the broader community. Only a limited number of institutions appear to be using capacity building strategies in relation to excluded communities.

As in other sectors, funding changes and new funding initiatives have been introduced to encourage institutions to extend their activities in local communities. In 1995-98, the Higher Education Funding Council for England (HEFCE) provided funds for non-award-bearing continuing education (NABCE) and the availability of a non-accredited budget enabled a number of institutions to develop innovative provision in their local areas.

There is now formula funding to widen participation in mainstream and to monitor participation by postcodes. Institutions which recruit and retain students who require strategies such as outreach initiatives and support receive funding premiums with special funding allocations weighted towards low-income and disabled students. Since October 1999, all HE institutions in England have been required to produce strategic statements and plans relating to widening participation as part of their corporate strategy. These will be monitored on an annual basis and linked to the provision of funding

Special funding has also been allocated for building partnerships between HEIs and other further and higher institutions, schools and community organisations. This is aimed at meeting local or regional needs and promoting longer-term institutional commitment to widening participation. Institutions are also expected to organise special recruitment schemes including outreach activities and summer schools.

These developments, combined with growing pressure on the sector to play a greater local and regional role, have led to the development and expansion of different forms of outreach activity in a number of universities, although this is still often peripheral to other means of attracting new student groups such as compact arrangements and summer schools.

Despite the recent changes in funding, however, some analysts perceive universities' role in local communities as still relatively weak and restricted to providing conventional types of courses that have failed to attract people in the past.

Many universities have been successful in their bids to the Widening Participation Special Funding Programme 1989-99. Some of them illustrate how universities have woken up to the needs of the community and users of education and training, which is a welcome if late development, largely engendered by funding pushes. However, it seems a lot of the successful bids do not really focus on equality and social inclusion. Rather typically, they are about encouraging wider participation in the same kind of curriculum albeit adapted. Some critics have even described it as a watered-down curriculum which, if it is, does not respect and value the learners in the community the programmes are seeking to attract....Often widening participation is perceived as developing more of the same type of education and training opportunity which has clearly not been able to address the needs of all learners in the past. (Sharma and Selway, 2000: 10-11)

On the other hand, some institutions have developed major community development strategies:

The University of Leeds is the lead-agency and Accountable Body for a countywide partnership involving community and voluntary groups, local authorities and other education providers....Similar or related initiatives have been developed by a number of both old and new universities including Sussex, Swansea, Bangor and Sheffield Hallam. The University of the Valleys in South Wales has been particularly well documented. (Ward and Steele, 1999: 196)

A number of other institutions have also made considerable efforts to reach their local communities as illustrated below:

- **The University of Lincolnshire and Humberside** is targeting rural communities and setting up a network of education advisers in regional access centres. The network will target second chance learners and those with limited access to learning due to isolation.
- **The University of Birmingham** is providing programmes for Pakistani and Bangladeshi women at community-based centres.
- **The University of East London** has a new Docklands campus and an outreach shop, in partnership with Barking College, which provides guidance.
- **London Guildhall University** has been working with the Bengali community for some years and is increasing work targeted at young working-class men as well as other local groups.
- **Leeds and Leeds Metropolitan Universities** have formed a community-based adult guidance network in inner-city Leeds in collaboration with the local authority and other post 16 providers.
- **Six universities in London** are working collaboratively to develop a framework to increase the participation of both young and mature people from ethnic minority and

lower socio-economic groups across east and north-east London. One of the areas identified for development is community outreach.

- **The School of Continuing Education at the University of Nottingham** is working in day centres with seriously disabled students and those with visual impairment and mental health difficulties. The subjects studied are chosen in consultation with students. In the three years to 1999, 400 people attended courses. Most were aged over 40 and included adults disabled from birth and those who have acquired a disability.

The NABCE programme referred to earlier generated a variety of outreach projects. A number of these were targeted at specific groups or geographical areas and some were designed to widen participation in particular curriculum areas:

Bolton IHE used the HEFCE funding for an Access Bus which goes into local communities and encourages groups to take first steps back into education. The **University of Essex** has delivered programmes for retired people in residential homes and sheltered accommodation; the **University of Sussex** has been running programmes on a deprived estate in Hastings, with additional funds generated from other sources; the **University of Leeds** has been providing a part-time, community-based programme for disadvantaged people from inner-city Muslim communities (particularly Bangladeshi and Pakistani women) which offers them a pathway into higher education.

Some of the larger widening provision projects funded by the NABCE programme employed a range of outreach strategies and targeted a number of disparate groups.

The project at **Sheffield Hallam University** involved six projects, all of which aimed to extend opportunities to, and extend the university's engagement with, different communities. Outreach activities included a guidance initiative (working with local guidance providers, equipping local communities to access information through IT); work with local parents and children; work with the WEA to develop an industrial museum as a centre for the study of science, technology and social history for local schools and unemployed adults; a Black Student Development Project (including a mentoring network for black young people and activities to introduce young black people to the university); involvement in the Coalfields Education Project in collaboration with Northern College to encourage adults with few qualifications to return to learning and engage in community regeneration. Through these initiatives:

there has been a gradual shift within the {University} Access and Guidance Service towards widening provision through grassroots activities, with a stronger, intrinsic emphasis on community and social regeneration. Involvement in these activities enabled the University to draw down funding from other sources for work in local communities.' (McNair, 1999: 16-17)

Use of higher education students as mentors and role models

Evaluation of the NABCE programme (McNair, 1999) found that an 'outstanding' feature of the most innovative projects was the use of existing students as mentors, tutors, outreach workers and researchers, who could act as role models and build links between communities and the institution. In Sunderland local mature graduates were recruited as staff in a project to develop a strategy for regeneration of the Ford and Pennywell estates. Thames Valley University trained undergraduates from ethnic minority communities to work as outreach workers with ethnic minority residents in Slough. These acted as role models and interpreters and helped to recruit participants to learning activities in the community. Student groups were also linked to staff at the School of Health Sciences, who were engaged in research into the health issues of specific minority communities:

The project gave researchers and their subjects direct access to each other, gave a particularly isolated group of non-participants access to the resource of the university, strengthened the skills of existing undergraduates, and provided a means of sharing knowledge between community and academe on its own doorstep. (McNair, 1999, 46)

As in further education, encouraging local people to train as learning champions, signposters or ambassadors is a growing form of outreach activity. The core idea of the Outreach in Salford Project, for example – a partnership between the University of Salford, Salford College and the local adult guidance service – is for local adult learners to provide information and advice to other local people.

In some areas, outreach activities have developed in response to particular economic and social circumstances, as in the example below:

The Community University of the Valleys grew out of the community-based partnership work developed by the Valleys' Initiative for Adult Education (VIAE) and the Dove Workshop at Banwen, following the coalfield crisis in the South West Valleys in the 1980s. The Department of Adult Continuing Education at the University of Wales, Swansea, collaborated with these networks in setting up access, women's training and guidance initiatives. Subsequently, the Community Access Movement in the South-Western Valleys was launched in 1990 and in 1993, the first Community University of the Valleys provision was offered at Banwen in the Dulais Valley. The aim was to address the needs of particular targeted groups: the long-term unemployed, disabled people and women returners. Learners were offered return to learn courses, ICT, interest-based courses and access provision supported by on-site childcare and transport. These programmes could lead to part-time degree programmes. The initiative later expanded to include partnership with the Open University and the University of Glamorgan and, in 1998, the first community-based CUV part-time degree students graduated. More centres are being developed and this way of attracting new students to HE has been adopted by other universities in Wales (Francis, 1999).

Local authorities

After a period in which community-based work diminished due to the S2-NS2 funding divide, a range of funding initiatives, such as the Adult and Community Learning Fund (ACLF), Project 99 (involving small sums to LEAs for widening participation activities) and the DfEE Laptops initiative, have encouraged an expansion of outreach work and prompted local education authorities to re-engage in innovative ways of working in the community. For example:

Following the introduction of the Laptops initiative, **Hampshire County Council** bought some laptops which will be placed in rural pubs and a development officer will work with volunteers in helping local people to use them. Six landlords have already signed up for the scheme and it is anticipated that the laptops will prove a valuable community resource for both individuals and community groups.

Lifelong learning plans and partnerships have also generated new community-based activity. For the year 1999-2000, the DfEE made £9m available through the Standards Fund, on a matched funding basis, to support LEAs in promoting lifelong learning in partnership with other bodies and in line with the principles set out in *The Learning Age* (DfEE, 1998a). The idea was to encourage a co-ordinated response using key local services to widen participation in learning. Analysis of LEA programmes of work in support of the development plans has identified many examples of work that could fall under the heading of outreach. These include, among others:

- a local learning shop in a local library which provides on-line open learning with tutor support and a telephone learning helpline linked to Learning Direct
- outreach guidance in community venues for socially excluded groups, and learning provision delivered in old peoples' homes and isolated estates
- the development of schools as community and lifelong learning centres
- basic skills and family learning in community settings
- a pilot to widen provision of information technology and learning opportunities for adults in libraries and schools
- the setting up of three community learning zones in areas where participation in organised learning is low
- targeted and piloted approaches for refugees, travellers, older adults, people not eligible for FEFC funds, Bangladeshi and other minority communities and unemployed men.

Outreach strategies are central to the lifelong learning plan of some local authorities. One example is Oxfordshire:

Oxfordshire County Council has a county-wide outreach team, funded from top-slicing the budget, as part of its lifelong learning plan. The team cover the county with each worker having a particular patch to work in. A county co-ordinator was appointed (at point 5) in June 1999, and subsequently, the full team of one FTE equivalent for each area, with additional workers in Oxford City and Banbury, were appointed on a year's (renewable) contract. All of these will receive accredited training.

Most of the outreach workers are women and all are local people who have had some experience of learning and voluntary community projects. Each member of the team is developing community specialisms (for example, working with Asian communities, rural communities, young mothers, older learners or other target priority groups). Their work is co-ordinated by the County Outreach Co-ordinator who is responsible to the Lifelong Learning Development Officer. Working with the lifelong learning plan and the county widening participation strategy, she oversees strategy countywide and represents the team at strategic planning.

Outreach is seen as an integral part of the service and there has been a deliberate attempt to reduce worker isolation. Each member of the team is based in an Adult Education Centre where they can relate directly to colleagues. There are regular team meetings as well as meetings with staff working in areas such as guidance, ABE, and learning difficulties.

The task of the team is to widen and help to sustain engagement in lifelong learning through such strategies as:

- identifying geographical areas and particular target groups for priority attention
- identifying where and how current provision fails to meet the needs of targeted groups and making recommendations for new and innovative provision
- making contact with targeted individuals and groups
- working with Community Education staff to ensure provision is developed
- initiating low-cost local informal provision
- developing meaningful cross-sector, interagency and inter-departmental partnerships
- working as a team to develop effective widening participation strategies and practice within the service
- using a variety of methods to encourage individuals or groups to develop or regain their interest in learning.

The outreach workers have access to an annual devolved budget to initiate low-cost or free informal initiatives in local venues. Although they have some autonomy in the use of funds, they also have specific group targets which are set for each area. In 1998-1999 the following target groups were given priority across the county:

- older learners
- some groups of women including lone parents
- people with few or no qualifications
- refugees and minority communities
- unskilled manual workers
- adults with mental illness
- offenders.

For the years 2000-2003, the County Widening Participation Partnership has set a target to increase take-up of learning opportunities by 30 per cent of 'non-participating' adults at levels 0-1 in LEA and Partnership institutions. The team will contribute to these targets but will also work to locally determined priorities. (Information supplied by Angela Wood, County Outreach Co-ordinator).

Another local authority which has incorporated outreach in its lifelong learning plan is East Sussex.

East Sussex County Council has an outreach project group as part of its lifelong development plan, whose remit is to: 'develop further projects that go out to "difficult to reach" groups across the county and encourage progression into further educational opportunities'. Within the context of the group, outreach is defined as: 'the creation of community-based learning initiatives that allow informed choices for current non participants'. Through such means the group wishes to widen participation, to develop new strategies, to use other methods such as informal learning, to recognise the value of off-site learning and non-accredited work, to build capacity for communities and individuals, to provide information and develop informed decision-making. (Information received from Mark Ravenhall, Adult Education Development Officer, East Sussex County Council).

Some local authorities' outreach activities include support to help community groups run their own programmes.

In **Bristol**, the Community Education service has been working with local community organisations and activists since 1993 on a wide range of community development projects and programmes. In its role as lifelong learning facilitator, the service provides annual funding to self-organised community groups who have been successful at designing and running their own community development learning programmes. An example is the West of England Coalition of Disabled People which has developed a range of empowerment courses for Disabled people. (Taylor, 2000: 18)

Voluntary organisations

Outreach practices are well established in the voluntary sector. Many voluntary organisations have always worked in an outreach way, taking services to the groups they serve and providing learning activities in response to expressed interests and needs. For example, the larger national voluntary organisations with a strong educational remit, such as the Workers' Educational Association and the National Federation of Women's Institutes, a significant outreach dimension to their work.

The WEA

WEA provision is defined within three categories: workplace learning, general programmes and community learning which involves provision aimed at specific groups or locations (there are 17 target groups). According to a national WEA officer, it is this dimension of WEA work that might best be described as outreach, although:

> *If you take a methodological point of view, everything the WEA does is outreach. From a political point of view, outreach is the targeted work. This is mostly delivered by professional staff (tutor organisers) rather than branches. Their job descriptions are to develop particular provision areas either in specific curriculum areas (e.g. ESOL) or for recognised target group, although in many cases it has outside funding therefore has a limited shelf life.*

A recent analysis of WEA partnerships (Ford and Jackson, 1999) confirmed the extent to which the Association is committed to working in a community-oriented way:

> *Education is taken out to the learners. Local communities are supported and encouraged to become involved in the administration of projects and gradually to take responsibility for their own learning... The WEA sees genuinely student-centred approaches as critical to the inclusion and engagement of many more individuals and communities in lifelong learning.* (p. 10)

The study found that the Association caters for the learning needs of a large number of target groups including:

- women
- families with no previous tradition of learning wanting to know how to support their children's education
- ethnic minority groups
- people recovering from mental illness
- adults with special learning needs
- gypsics and travellers
- people with various disabilities, including the deaf and the visually impaired
- the frail elderly
- communities where large scale industries have shut down (eg coal and steel closures)
- remote rural communities.

The authors of the study report that, in reaching and working with these groups, the Association has developed considerable experience and expertise in essential outreaching practices such as:

- building and sustaining relationships with local community groups
- identifying local community learning needs and responding appropriately
- negotiating with students, and encouraging and supporting them to become involved in the design and delivery of their educational

programmes, and gradually to take fuller responsibility for their own learning

- capacity-building – equipping local community groups with the skills to sustain and take forward existing provision, and at the same time to contribute towards the development and enrichment of their own communities
- providing gateways to learning.

The WEA's experience is that short courses which provide tasters to learning, and help to instil confidence in the student that she/he has the ability to learn, can be more successful in providing gateways to further education than longer term programmes including those which are accredited. (p. 7)

An example of WEA outreach work

The Western District has been awarded a Lottery grant for a three-year development project with women in refuges and hostels on the south coast. This has enabled the WEA to work in partnership with housing associations in women's refuges in Bournemouth and Weymouth, in flats for single mothers and in a hostel in Poole which provides self-catering accommodation for homeless single women. The project has developed a programme to help the women increase their self-esteem and self-confidence, acquire new skills and access education, training and employment when they move on to permanent accommodation. The courses provided (which have been suggested by housing association staff and the women themselves) have included DIY, Emergency First Aid, Self-Defence, Crafts and 'Make Your Experience Count'. These have been delivered in a secure and supportive environment where there is help with childcare. Although there have been some difficulties and tutors have needed to be adaptable and flexible, the results have justified the efforts:

All tutors involved in the project have to be police-checked, and they have to be flexible – the rooms available for classes are less than ideal, and there are interruptions from other residents, and from children. Attendance is erratic and unpredictable, and the mood of the refuge and of individual women can change from week to week. But the tutors are enthusiastic and committed, and the rewards are tremendous. At the first session of a DIY course, one very withdrawn, timid woman successfully rewired a plug for the first time in her life and did it faster than anyone else. It had a powerful effect on her, and really made her day. She had discovered that she was good at something, and enjoyed a sense of achievement. A student from a 'Make Your Experience Count' course said that as a result of the course, she was jogging, swimming and eating more healthily. She wrote, 'I have been reading quite a few books; in fact, I can't stop reading – something I've not done before and it's making me a stronger person. Another thing is that I've become a lot more assertive and 1 won't allow myself to be talked into something that 1 don't want to do.' (Dowding, 1999: 45)

Public services

Libraries

Increased involvement in community-based activity is reflected in the work of public services. Public libraries, for example, were the most popular locations for the BBC *Computers Don't Bite* and *Webwise* taster sessions and many have become involved in encouraging lifelong learning. Some now have lifelong learning managers and about 80 per cent have open learning centres. They have also become increasingly involved in different forms of outreach activity. The Community Services Group of the Library Association, which works to combat disadvantage and to promote equal access for all communities to library and information services, is active in providing services for cultural and racial minorities, people with disabilities, retired people, the unemployed, single parents and the homeless, and is also involved in health issues and community development. Every library authority has a housebound users service for hospitals, prisons and other institutions and some take services to day centres and residential homes for old peoples. The outreach dimension to library work has been given added impetus by recent funding initiatives. Some projects funded by the National Year of Reading, for example, have involved outreach to Travellers, schools, pre-school playgroups, disaffected youth, people with disabilities and people in shopping centres. Manchester libraries used a local basketball team to promote reading.

A growing dimension of library services is provision of access to ICT. There are plans to train librarians in Internet skills and link all UK public libraries in the to the Internet by 2002. Some are already heavily involved:

In **Gloucestershire**, the county library service put a PC in the parish hall in a small village in response to requests for internet access; in **Rotherham**, the library worked with youth and community workers on an estate to create an electronic community magazine. This won a Library Changes Lives Award in 1998. **Croydon Libraries**, which have a Housebound User Group ('Huggies'), have provided some housebound people in the area with a PC, a modem and training in how to use technology. Information is provided via websites so that even when the library is shut, the community will be able to obtain library and information services.

BBC Education

BBC Education is another service which has developed outreach activities in order to connect more with its audiences, to encourage people to continue learning beyond programmes and move them on from passive to more active learning. According to a staff member: *In the past the BBC did less to connect with its audiences. Now it has woken up to the need to communicate with them more effectively, not only in education but other areas.*

A team of 10 Learning Link Advisers (LLAs), based in the Department of Learning Support, work in an outreach capacity across the UK. Recruited for their skills, experience and local knowledge, their work is strongly campaign-oriented and all have developed their own local and regional networks. These are both general networks and specific ones for each learning campaign. The LLAs identify providers in their regions who are prepared to act as partners for specific learning initiatives and education campaign such as *Computers Don't Bite, Webwise* and *History 2000.* The campaign *Computers Don't Bite* was particularly successful at engaging organisations and individuals in supporting regional activities. The campaign had free taster courses provided by a range of partners in diverse local venues. This was found to be a very effective way of reaching people and where appropriate, subsequent campaigns such as *Webwise* have followed that model.

Each education campaign or programme usually has accompanying learning materials that people can send for, and viewers and listeners are also referred to a phone line (sometimes Learndirect) which will inform them on where they can develop their interest further or find a taster course locally. For example, the recent campaign to encourage young people to get involved in sports, Get your Kit On, is linked with free regional sports tasters.

A numeracy campaign launched in May 2000 aims to raise awareness of the importance of basic numeracy skills and help parents of primary school children to gain a better understanding of the maths their children are learning at school has. The campaign has a CD-ROM to give parents the chance to improve their basic numeracy skills at local drop-in centres. For this campaign LLAs will contact partners such as primary schools, family learning centres, libraries, basic skills providers, organisations providing services to parents of children aged 5-11, homework clubs, work-based learning centres and organisations providing out-of-school support activities.

As well as finding partners for various campaigns, the LLAs engage in strategic local activity, working with local structures, key education providers, libraries, regional museum councils and local forums and networks such as Open College Networks, lifelong learning partnerships, University for Industry groups and Adult Learners' Week committees. The team meets with campaign managers at the Department for Learning Support for two days every two months for updates, sharing and pooling experience.

The LLA scheme appears to have had a very positive impact in the areas where the advisors operate:

It's obviously more effective to have someone on the ground than trying to achieve the same results remotely from London. A human face makes a huge difference particularly with non-traditional providers.

External evaluation showed that providers and other intermediaries who have had contact with LLAs are likely to be aware of the range of the BBC's educational output and services, likely to take part in BBC campaigns, likely to play an active part in them.

The BBC is also engaging with local organisations and communities in its work with libraries. BBC Education and the Library Association have joined in a strategic partnership in an attempt to link broadcasting and libraries and use them to promote learning. Some libraries are acting as BBC 'outposts', providing referrals to learning opportunities and feedback to the BBC.

*　*　*

The small number of examples outlined above suggest that there has been a significant shift towards outreach forms of working, much of it, in the education sector at least, encouraged by new funding initiatives put in place to increase lifelong learning and combat social exclusion. Current educational outreach activities typically take a number of forms – the targeting of specific groups or specific geographical areas; the extension of mainstream courses into the community and the development of new curricula in response to identified demand and needs. The aims are usually to engage groups identified as economically, socially and educationally disadvantaged in learning, to make them aware of existing provision, to provide learning activities to new locations such as housing estates as a stepping stone to mainstream programmes, and – a relatively new but growing activity – to build local capacity by training local people as animateurs, signposters, learning champions or community change agents.

Some of the most effective outreach initiatives involve extensive inter-agency and cross-sectoral networking. The Valleys Initiative for Adult Education (VIAE), for example, has networks across the region, encouraging community enterprise, equal partnerships and community-based learning. It provides guidance on policy issues and supports outreach organisations involved in delivering learning in deprived valley communities. It currently also provides training to groups to train community agents of change.

A number of interrelated factors explain the extent and nature of outreach activities in which institutions and organisations engage – the type of institution and its geographical and demographic location; its history, tradition and mission; the way it is funded; the urgency of other agendas and priorities and the availability of dedicated budgets or special funding; the extent of managerial support and commitment to community-based work; and the motivation and enthusiasms of particular members of staff.

In some organisations and institutions outreach is a central concept, integral to their mission, and is strongly supported by senior managers; in others it constitutes only a small strand of overall work and is marginal to other priorities. However, just to describe an institution as engaging in outreach is to gloss over the variety and complexities of the work and the wide range of issues it raises. These will be explored in subsequent chapters.

CHAPTER THREE

The implications of doing outreach

'Disadvantage'

The evidence from current practice suggests that 'outreach', like 'community', has become irrevocably and perhaps irretrievably associated with the concept of disadvantage. This has been the case since the Russell Report (1973) identified non-participants in adult education as suffering from various kinds of disadvantage and this connotation has been reinforced in the wording of much current policy and funding documents. While one cannot question the good intentions behind the directing of outreach approaches towards those groups and areas identified as most socially, economically and educationally deprived, the effect can be to 'pathologise' the people concerned, to suggest that groups which may be very disparate all require the same approach, and even, ultimately, to stymie efforts to create a more radical and responsive overall education service. In their account of the history of outreach in the Inner London Education Authority (ILEA), Taubman and Cushman (1981) relate how the original intention to expand and democratise adult education for working-class Londoners was diluted and distorted: 'first [by] somewhat woolly notions of community, and then most seriously by the pathology of disadvantage' (p.45).

Taubman and Cushman (p. 46-47) describe how ILEA outreach workers were obliged to collude with the concept of disadvantage and to resort to special pleading 'in ever more heart-rending terms' to get the necessary resources for 'groups of ever more needy individuals'. They became 'fixers for ever more disparate groups', with their efforts concentrated on 'a rag-bag of disadvantaged groups whose only unifying factor seemed that they could be collectively categorised as deserving of charity'. According to this analysis, the opportunity to create a new kind of democratic and empowering education which would have a lasting impact on policy and mainstream practice in London was lost when ILEA Adult Education chose the easier, more traditional and less controversial path and:

> gratefully grasped the straw of disadvantage and substituted it for any real change of direction. The concept of disadvantage...fits a traditional model of liberal, paternal adult education far easier than the theories and practices that were being tentatively established in Liverpool. (p. 44)

If outreach is seen only, or principally, as a means of combating disadvantage, it may result in a blurring of the boundary between an education intervention and a social services one. It can also imply deficiencies in the people targeted. Reflecting on their experience as ILEA outreach workers in a paper aptly entitled 'The unease of the outreach worker', Nicholls and Murray (1981: 60) acknowledge the extent to which they were obliged to seek out 'needs, disadvantages, deficiencies and pathologies' which they were then expected to remedy through means such as tutor hours and class materials – 'in order to justify their activities in terms which 'harmonised with the felt expectations of us as the Authority's remedial/disadvantage workers (or social conscience?)'. This caused discomfort when they encountered groups who did not fit the pejorative labels and characteristics applied to them:

We are professionally at a loss if, encouraged to seek for deficiency, we find good humour, strengths and resiliences, expressed wants which may not particularly match what we have to offer, and resourcefulness counter-balancing disadvantage.'

Moreover, in their experience, it was never the most disadvantaged groups who were targeted, but those who were easiest to reach and work with:

If we are genuinely assessing priority needs in different geographical areas of Inner London, why do we all come up with such similar formulae – e.g. activities for mothers and toddlers? Yes, we consider this group is a priority group throughout the Inner City; but it is also an acceptable group that is relatively easily found and gathered together, fairly highly motivated and on the whole attractive and lively! Do we give lesser priority to groups who are less easily identified, contacted and organised, less highly motivated and less attractive e.g. down-and-outs? (1981: 60)

In their joint soul-searching, Nicholls and Murray (p57) describe how the stress of trying simultaneously to meet community demands and work within bureaucratic structures prevented them from recognising:

the growth of parallel provision for the 'disadvantaged' as the second class system that it really was. In order to cope with the demands of day to day work we accepted {measures and processes} which institutionalised the notion that Adult Education was a social service for those with special needs, rather than a right for any adult who chose to follow it.

However, they also accept that their role in controlling access to educational resources entailed a moral responsibility which they had not fully recognised the implications of:

How far do we ourselves monopolise access, by allowing access only where we think fit? Alternatively, how far do we see ourselves involved in participative education, making quite clear what resources are available and consulting on ways in which they might be used.

Although the ILEA outreach work was conducted over 20 years ago, this retrospective analysis encapsulates some of the dilemmas facing providers and outreach workers today. It demonstrates how easy it can be to fall into the trap of imposing one's own values and preferences in outreach work, and using outreach as a remedial rather than transformative tool, which results in the work being automatically perceived as low level. A related pitfall, reinforced by the wording of many current policy and funding documents, is to treat all the groups identified as 'disadvantaged' as though they all have the same needs and therefore require the same approach. But, as noted by one outreach worker, it is a mistake to assume that a single model will work in all areas.

Moreover, as several outreach workers reported to this study, many people do not see themselves as belonging to the neat categories of disadvantage to which they are assigned and do not congregate in groups characterised by labels such as 'lone parents', 'the homeless' or 'the unemployed', thus they cannot easily be contacted:

> *Whilst some of the people you aim to reach may already attend another group or make use of a particular building which gives you a focus to start, the people who really need your help are often scattered through the community.* (Outreach worker)

Targeting

It is nevertheless widely agreed that outreach effort must involve some targeting, otherwise it could be ineffective:

> *We have to work out where we can really get best value. Small amounts of time in too many areas are much less effective. We have to work out where we will have most impact. Workers have to be ruthless in the time they spend.* (BBC Education officer)

> *The problem is that HEIs are so geographically widespread with huge communities to cover. They have to build too many relations. It's more appropriate to focus the work on specific communities. We have to change the idea that outreach is going out to everybody. Now it's more targeted.* (HE project officer)

Outreach workers cannot be expected to deal with all problems of disadvantage and under-representation and it is usually found to be more manageable to target people who fall into various sub-groups. However, there are a number of moral and ethical questions involved in targeting.

Outreach strategies that are not linked to a specific curriculum area (such as people requiring ESOL) or location (such as action zones) need to focus on specific groups or geographical areas. But how are these to be selected? Who or what determines the choice of where to target outreach energies and resources? As Nicholls and Murray admit (1981: 57): 'in allocating scarce resources to one group, by definition we deprive other groups; but we rarely consider this, political, dimension of our work'.

Targeted educational outreach activity is usually based on a specific location (an estate); on group characteristics such as age, race, gender, disability or activity (for example, people in low paid occupations), or on perceived or expressed needs. Some groups by virtue of their circumstances specifically require outreach approaches – elderly people, those who are homebound, people with disabilities; people in day centres, prisons, etc. Some education providers have missions or specialisms that lead them naturally to work with certain groups. Oaklands College, for example, has a tradition of working with people with profound and multiple learning difficulties. However, in other institutions, targeting decisions may depend less on tradition or identified need than on institutional or personal value systems:

The choice the worker or educator makes on how to use the time, money and other resources available will reflect the worker's personal value system or the norms of his or her employing body.

The decision as to which of several potential individuals or groups to assist cannot be taken solely on mechanistic, techniques-orientated grounds. It is a second order decision which will depend on the values, ethics and moral stance of the educator. (Brookfield, 1983: 68 and 199)

If outreach work is defined by location, difficult choices still arise. As observed earlier, any area or segment of the population may contain a plethora of different groups, each with different interests and priorities which means, as Watson and Tyers (1998) point out, that local sensitivities must be taken into account: if outreach workers are associated with one particular group they may become the object of suspicion to others. Trotman and Pudner (1998: 48-49) make the same point in relation to projects on housing estates in Swansea:

Activity in one part of the ward cannot be allowed to alienate another section of the community. Educational activity must, wherever possible, be seen as a response to all members of the wider community and operating across perceived community boundaries. Otherwise, there is a very real risk that the providing organisation will be seen as favouring one group of residents as opposed to another.

In the work with tenants on an estate in Trafford described in Chapter 2, conflicts between different groups limited both involvement in and the impact of the initiative. As the project worker commented: 'One of the first things you learn in a community-based project is that there are tensions and conflicts in any community'.

Thus the selection of groups to work with places a heavy burden of responsibility on outreach workers who have to conduct a delicate balancing act in order to be seen as fair and impartial and to avoid the appearance of favouring one group at the expense of another. They may also experience tension between their desire to help particular groups of people and their professional requirement to uphold the values and interests of the institution they work for. As one commented: 'everything we do has to be college beneficial'. However, targeting decisions are also driven by policy, and the current availability of mainstream funding allocations and funding for specific disadvantaged areas or under-represented groups inevitably encourages institutions to target their outreach activities primarily at the groups and areas prioritised. An unforeseen development arising from this is the problem one informant to this study described as 'over-fishing'. Some geographical locations which have been recognised as priority areas are attracting a variety of different and often unconnected regeneration funding streams. This sometimes leads to an over-concentration of interventions in these areas and the neglect of others with a lower profile which may be equally deserving of attention. A number of the people who supplied information for this study expressed concern that regeneration and other funding is being channelled continually into the same locations, amounting to the creation of fashions in bidding culture: As one commented:

> some geographical areas are fashionable and attract funding so everyone now puts them in their bids! A lot of regeneration funding is flying around and the first thing that people do is development work, often in areas which have been completely over-funded.

The dangers inherent in this trend were identified by informants to this study not only as neglect of some areas, but incoherence (lack of connection between initiatives), duplication of effort, and, sometimes, resentment on the part of those with a history of working in the targeted locations and territorial disputes. As Watson and Tyers (1998) observe, interventions by an outside agency in an area where local groups have been working for some time can lead to suspicion and conflict. If there are other adult education providers working in the same patch, outreach workers may be open to accusations of trespassing. Several of the people consulted during the course of this study had experienced or heard of misunderstandings and conflicts between different agencies working in the same areas or with the same groups of people:

When we did outreach we never knew who was doing bits in the same place, so there'd be all these people from Social Services, Housing and other departments, as well as us, descending on those poor people.

It's always the same areas. People think they need to go back to some places without asking the people who know them. They don't consult the grassroots practitioners who say 'we've been here for donkeys' years and now you're coming in'.

The voluntary sector fears that the college is taking over and moving into their patch and that it can do this because its got heaps of money.

The over-fishing of some communities is a real problem. Postcodes risk over-fishing. Grassroots workers can be pissed off: too many people coming onto their patch, no consultation and co-ordination. There should be far more joined-up thinking by various sectors when it comes to outreach.

Networking with other agencies

Such territorial problems are common and probably somewhat unavoidable in outreach work especially when a range of different sectors are involved. Writing about a further education outreach project funded by the former REPLAN programme, Kinneavy (1989: 71) related that other agencies perceived the college as having 'imperialist' tendencies:

One AE organiser told the research worker, 'You are treading on my toes.' A local worker for a national charity operating a community-based resource centre in a severely deprived area refused the college its crèche facility for outreach purposes, commenting, 'I don't see any reason for the voluntary sector to underwrite the statutory sector.' These comments tended to reflect a wider sense of unease within some sections of community-based groups, especially in the early stages of the project.

In order to gain the co-operation of other agencies working in an area, outreach workers need to engage in preliminary dialogue with local organisations, to reassure them that the service is intended to complement – not compete with – their work and to establish a relationship of mutual trust and co-operation.

It is an important principle in outreach work [to] establish co-operative links with other providers of services who are working in the same geographic area. Many providers have long histories of educational involvement in local communities which may be formally established, as with AE and the WEA, or informally organised by voluntary associations, who nevertheless contribute equally to local AE activities. Colleges, by contrast, have little experience of community education outside the institution, and it is understandable that college outreach initiatives might be seen to some extent to be trespassing. Contact and communication between the college and the various other providers becomes important if suspicion and distrust are to be overcome and fears of territorial encroachment are to be allayed. (Kinneavy, 1989: 71)

Inter-agency partnerships

The establishment of inter-agency partnerships and co-operative networks is a strong theme in current social and educational policy. They are a crucial plank of any outreach work and the vital to its effectiveness. However, genuine partnerships are not easy to form and sustain and some of the outreach workers consulted during this study had experienced some resistance in their institutions to forming the kind of good working relationships that would make their role easier:

> *For outreach to be effective, I think what one's talking about is developing a relationship with other organisations, community groups and communities that can be sustained overt a long period of time. I think this is incredibly important for a big education institution, but they don't take it on board. A lot of the successful work we've done is only because of the sustained nature of our relationship within the community over a long period.* (HE project officer)

Informants to this study referred to difficult working relationships among some of the agencies involved in lifelong learning partnerships, a common complaint being that the larger, more powerful institutions tended to ignore or ride rough-shod over smaller partners. In their study of WEA partnerships, Ford and Jackson (1999) list some of the problems staff encountered with further education colleges in some districts. Examples cited include: colleges taking over successful WEA courses; refusing to allow the WEA to use college premises even where there had previously been a long-standing agreement; questioning the necessity of entering into partnerships with the WEA and the voluntary sector; and being unco-operative during partnership and other meetings.

Kinneavy (1989: 73) suggests that for educational outreach purposes, the functions and purposes of networking and collaboration arrangements between providers should be: to share information, experience and resources in order to avoid duplication and competition; to recognise the contribution that can be made by different agencies; to identify gaps in provision and unmet and developing needs; to identify available provision and progression routes and to establish mechanisms for guidance and referral. Unless all relevant agencies work together to achieve these aims, outreach efforts may result in unnecessary duplication or failure.

Identifying community needs

A frequently stated aim of outreach activities is to meet local community 'needs'. But who identifies or determines those needs? And what if there are competing or conflicting needs? As Brookfield (1983: 68), who has considered this issue in depth, argues, community-based workers sometimes receive conflicting requests from different groups:

A problem...is the way in which it is assumed that the needs of all members of a community can be met at any one time. This ignores the possibility that there will be times when the community worker or community educator is faced with requests for assistance from different groups whose interests are diametrically opposed.

Brookfield also points out that perceptions of community needs are often subjective and prescriptive, with educators making value judgements based on their own perceptions and prejudices:

The concept of community needs is highly questionable. What are usually offered as examples of community needs tend to be one person's...prescription as to the kind of community change he or she considers desirable. (p.68)

He makes a distinction between felt needs – those perceived and expressed by people themselves – and prescribed needs – those which we *think* people have and which we believe should be met. This view of needs leads to services being provided for people for their own good, regardless of their own wishes and preferences.

A prescriptive need is present whenever an educator, community developer or any external agency decides that adults are in a state of inadequacy, deficiency or inferiority when compared to states which the external educator decides are preferable...Felt needs are of a different order from prescribed needs. On the one hand are simple expressions of desire by clients, on the other lie educators' prescriptions of the kinds of skills and competencies which they believe adults ought to acquire. These latter skills and competencies are diagnosed as essential irrespective of whether or not students see them as necessary. (Brookfield, 1983: 129-130)

Consulting with community representatives is a common way of identifying felt learning needs but this process is often tokenistic. There is also a risk that the people consulted may have a partial or inaccurate view of local needs and priorities:

To assert that community needs can somehow be synthesised from a number of individual felt needs is another familiar misconception. The best that one can hope for is that a community need as perceived by the educator reflects the majority preference of the inhabitants within an area. (Brookfield, 1983: 68)

Most outreach workers automatically consult existing networks in the patches where they operate, as well as 'key' people who are in touch with local issues. If these are the right networks and the right people, this is by far the most effective way of identifying local interests and needs. But sometimes there are no local networks in place and it is easier to ask professionals who are already working in the area for their perceptions of local needs. However, they too may have a limited or partial view of what these are ('it is easy to make sweeping statements about "the community" based on contact with just a few people' Smith, 1994: 156), or they may have values and agendas that do not coincide with those of local people:

> *[we] tend to take short cuts in forming impressions of a local neighbourhood, by consulting local people who may in some ways be regarded as 'key' in local community networks. We consult those who may broadly be described as professional social and community workers and educationalists, who have day-by-day contacts in their working capacity with local residents; but, in doing so, we are well aware that their assessment of local educational needs will be slanted by their own personal, professional and service perspectives, and are probably not a true reflection of local opinion at all.* (Nicholls and Murray, 1981: 58)

Identifying and responding to local interests and learning needs is therefore fraught with moral and ethical problems. Brookfield described the dilemma for educators as an attempt to walk the notoriously difficult tightrope between providing sensitive assistance in the articulation of genuinely felt needs and 'falling prey to a benevolent authoritarianism'.

Responding to identified needs

Whichever model of outreach is operated – whether a supply-led model, in which an education provider wishes to offer existing programmes to unreached sections of the population, or a demand-led model in which a provider responds to new learning interests – the community consultation process has important implications for the providing organisation. One of these, as Gilman (1992: 45) points out, is that outreach work may reveal views and perceptions of an institution and its services that managers do not want to hear, even when activities have been initiated precisely in order to find out why people are non-participants and what their preferences are! Another implication is that when new learning needs are identified through consultation, a provider needs to be able to address them in order to maintain credibility, and address them promptly, not in six months' time. ILEA Community education workers (Southwark Institute, 1981: 20, 21) make the point that, however articulate a worker may be, in a practical outreach situation, his or her success depends ultimately on the effectiveness of practical service delivery.

[Outreach] must be planned...in terms of...the capacity of the Authority to respond, with actual resources, to the ideas thrown up. It must be squarely faced that the exercise of going about interviewing people, explaining about the local adult education service, and asking them what they want, may result in them actually telling us! One of the likely outcomes of such a survey is that it will create new demands from individuals and groups wishing to use adult education resources. If sufficient resources are not forthcoming to match these demands, at least in part, it can only result in the Service being discredited in the eyes of would-be local consumers.

Several informants to this study made similar points:

If a dialogue is opened up between providers and people not using their services then those organisations and institutions should try and respond to the ideas generated. (FE manager)

Quite a lot of widening participation funding is focused on the demand side – the pre-entry bit, raising awareness, but not on the supply side. (HE project officer)

The evidence collected for this study suggests that institutional outreach is often conducted more with the aim of raising awareness of mainstream services than with a view to responding to new needs. Although there may be token dialogue, this often consists of asking people to state their learning preferences rather than engaging them in discussions about their experience and concerns. Many people have a restricted view of learning as something that is subject – and classroom – based, and if asked what they want to learn, will suggest subjects that are non-threatening and familiar, that they know are available or those they feel are 'acceptable', none of which may be what they really want. Outreach workers therefore stress that the consultation process should not be a simple matter of asking what people want to learn but an in-depth dialogue which allows interests, needs and priorities to emerge in a way that might not happen if they were presented with a traditional, pre-packaged 'menu' to choose from. It is commonplace that people are more likely to engage and continue in learning when programmes are designed in direct response to their interests and priorities.

Within the best traditions of adult education, we have to learn to consult more fully on an equal basis, treat our consumers as adults and allow them to set our agenda with us....we need to learn and relearn and go on working at the whole process of developing participative consultation with our potential consumers, as adults, in an equal partnership. (Nicholls and Murray, 1981: 60)

[The community development curriculum] differs from mainstream adult and further education provision in significant ways. Community members are

recognised as the true experts in relation to their experiences and situation and are actively engaged in all programme decision making processes. Also, with a focus on process instead of content alone, the curriculum is allowed to emerge in the process of action. In other words, learning takes place through the provision of integrated support and informal dialogue with community members, leading to local development work and action, rather than the more traditional implementation of pre-pack aged, off-the-shelf classroom provision. (Taylor, 2000: 18)

Whatever the initial focus of any learning programmes developed, different interests usually soon emerge. Thus outreach workers should keep abreast of changing interests, aspirations and needs.

[The community development curriculum] differs from mainstream adult and further education provision in significant ways. Community members are recognised as the true experts in relation to their experiences and situation and are actively engaged in all programme decision making processes. Also, with a focus on process instead of content alone, the curriculum is allowed to emerge in the process of action. In other words, learning takes place through the provision of integrated support and informal dialogue with community members, leading to local development work and action, rather than the more traditional implementation of pre-pack aged, off-the-shelf classroom provision. (Taylor, 2000: 18)

Community-based outreach programmes should therefore involve more than the transfer into community venues of pre-packaged programmes which have little connection or relevance to the lives people lead. As Nicholls and Murray (1981) have pointed out, if providers fail to act on the suggestions generated through community consultation and provide activities that are relevant to people's interests, the professional integrity of the worker may be called into question. More than once the OECD (1999) report on overcoming exclusion stresses the importance of allowing people to define and develop their own learning interests:

learning becomes effective and learners show most motivation when they see clear links between the learning and their practical needs and when they see possibilities for transforming their lives individually or collectively. This means that the learning offered must be more than compartmentalised sets of skills or knowledge. (pp. 38-39)

The current discourses around social exclusion tend to view employment as the overriding solution to disadvantage regardless of its cause, and there is consequently a tendency to offer outreach learning opportunities that ostensibly further this goal. However, Stuart (1995: 203) argues that a broader approach is required which caters for the needs of diverse groups of learners:

The debate over skills versus liberal adult education is a limited one. While offering opportunities to some, both discourses exclude certain individuals and groups from learning what they wish to study. Both discourses 'imagine' a social identity for particular groups in society and 'imagine' a particular identity for 'education'.... Through challenging who has access to the range of educational opportunities, the distinctions between learning for leisure and learning for work diminish. Groups of learners which have been excluded from education through a social acceptance of one discourse of education in the past are looking for an education discourse...that will meet their needs and which may include instrumental skills for work as well as personal development study.

The identification of what is useful learning is often done as a group. Community-based learning is frequently a collective rather than an individual process, motivated by factors such as a need for information on local issues and concerns about health, safety, transport, the environment and children's development and welfare. Despite this, current policy still envisages education as a wholly individual process conducted in isolation from the family, social and community contexts in which people lead their lives. This is reflected in the practices of the (many) educational institutions which still regard outreach purely as a means of recruiting individuals to existing provision. In their account of a collaborative venture involving WEA learning groups being brought into a university, Tidswell and Warrender (1999: 11) comment:

Collective or group learning is a success story in the community yet HE predominantly focuses on the more traditional, individual learning path. In the feedback sessions it became clear that many students wanted to stay together and progress in their collective mode of learning.

However, an HE project officer pointed out that there is no point in raising awareness of existing provision among disadvantaged groups without also examining the ways in which providing agencies and institutions actually operate.

Changing institutional practice

To respond to new learning needs requires a leap of faith and risk-taking on the part of providers, as well as considerable flexibility, all of which may be incompatible with the way in which they habitually work. One adult education outreach worker interviewed during the course of this study voiced her frustration at centre heads' inability to work in non-traditional ways: 'they're stuck in the traditional format or model of delivery – repeats of courses during standard terms, two hours a night. This doesn't suit the new learners coming in'.

This is a well-established contradiction in institutional outreach. Back in the 1970s, ILEA outreach workers found that the rigidities in adult education structures and procedures meant they could only respond to expressed interests and requests within well-defined limits and resource categories such as tutor hours for 'acceptable' subjects, which may have been irrelevant or inappropriate the people concerned:

> *In our daily work we have been constantly trying to present AE in terms that encouraged people to use it, and then having to present to the Institutes activities and demands that were not compatible with their terms of reference (vocational versus non-vocational, panels, ratios, fees, enrolment procedures, etc. etc.)* (Nicholls and Murray, 1981: 57)

The ILEA outreach workers experienced difficulties in their attempts to fit the diverse groups and individuals with whom they were working into administrative 'pigeon holes and requirements' while having 'formidable misgivings' about the values on which these were based:

> *The tension has particularly been reflected in the long-running battle around the issue of 'educational standards' put forward by the inspectorate as having universal application [but] seen in the light of workers' experience to be only narrowly valid...The Service must continually ask itself whose side it is on; whether we wish to perpetrate administrative structures for their own sakes, or whether we should rather be searching out ways of introducing flexibilities to engage with the varieties of human experience encountered in Inner London.*
>
> *...Some of the fiercest struggles the workers had were...over standards of taste. 'Good' was the goal of the Inspectorate as defined in the most gender-stereotyped, white, middle-class way possible.* (Taubman and Cushman, 1981: 21, 23, 45)

As is often the case, the nature of, and possibilities presented by, educational outreach in ILEA were framed and determined by the political and professional values of the existing education system and providing institutes. The difficulty of bridging the gap between the flexibility of outreach work and the rigidity of bureaucratic procedures involved in education institutions is still a common problem faced by outreach workers who often find that their attempts to respond to identified learning needs and interests are hindered by the structures, practices and funding constraints of their employing institutions. As articulated by Stuart and Thomson (1995: 10-12), institutional values and practices strongly influence a huge part in the development of outreach activities, resulting frequently in a one-way process rather than a genuine engagement with local people:

> *Even when outreach work values the existing experiences and knowledge of particular communities and responds to stated needs, the assumed direction of the*

knowledge transfer, and the comparative power of the centre, will privilege and reproduce the prevailing forms of knowledge from the centre. By contrast, the centre's own educational assumptions may be relatively unaffected by the relationship...

We operate within professional languages and practices which limit and prescribe this engagement... Our base and grounding in professional practices can get in the way of education which relates to different people's experiences... As professional educators we sometimes find it difficult to see outside of our structures... Even when we try to work outside our institutional perspectives, the financial, procedural and political features of the institution limit what we can do.

It is not easy for institutions to relinquish professional domination of outreach developments, but the imposition of values and inflexible standards and practices on community-based work can prove a significant obstacle to its acceptability and effectiveness. Community interventions will only be effective if they are acceptable to and are sanctioned by the client group:

Institutional values may conflict with the values of the community in which the work is to take place. Institutional representatives with preconceived ideas about what people need or want may be deeply resented by that community. (REPLAN South and South West, 1989)

Thus, as Diamond (1999: 20) stresses, it is important for providers to recognise that: 'they are temporary visitors to these communities, not permanent fixtures, and the needs of the provider are secondary to the rights and demands of the communities'. Similarly, Gilman (1992: 10-11) argues:

It cannot be stressed enough that outreach work takes place on other people's territory. Outreach workers need to negotiate their way through the cultural norms and dominant ideologies of the target groups. Working in an outreach setting means that you enter the clients' world on their terms not yours.

Outreach settings

The places where local learning activities are delivered themselves deserve careful consideration. The estate agent mantra – 'location, location, location' – can also be applied to outreach and the importance, for new groups, of learning in a familiar setting near to their homes should not be underestimated. Many outreach workers have found that the location of learning is even more important than its focus. This is due not only to practical but to psychological and cultural factors. In some deprived areas, people are reluctant to go far beyond their familiar local boundaries – a fact that is recognised by experienced practitioners:

In inner-city areas only very local centres can help make education accessible to individuals and communities otherwise excluded by distance, transport or cultural barriers. (Fryer, 1997)

It can be years and years before they are ready to move out of those communities into somewhere else, or even to the community that's a mile down the road. (Wood, 2000)

Many analysts therefore advise that, in the early stages, outreach activities should involve and promote only local learning opportunities as there may be little interest in provision outside the immediate area.

Research conducted by the Further Education Funding Council for Wales (1999) found that, although costly, outreach provision delivered in a range of local sites to small numbers of learners was more effective than a single point of delivery because they were more closely associated with the community and not viewed as institutions. The selection of such venues can, however, present outreach workers with a number of problems. Watson and Tyers (1998) describe those faced by one demonstration outreach project that was seeking suitable local premises in which to offer guidance. Some of the proposed venues proved unsuitable (for example, a church that was only available during the evenings) and some groups that had offered premises eventually found that they were unable to co-operate because of changed circumstances. Other projects experienced problems arising from multiple use of premises. Some reported lack of co-operation and rivalries between different services using the same venue: 'in one extreme case a fist-fight broke out between two rival groups'. To deal with issues such as these requires considerable tact and diplomacy.

Watson and Tyers (1998) report that the difficulties involved in finding suitable premises led workers in some of the projects to consider taking services further away from the target communities in order to offer a more congenial setting. However:

the general conclusion has been that the latter can be hugely counter-productive, as residents are often unwilling or unable to leave their immediate vicinity to engage in activities of any nature. Whilst individuals will need to overcome these barriers at some point, the initial steps are almost definitely easier if taken locally The only exception has been where clients have preferred to travel beyond their estate when they wish to discuss personal issues of a sensitive nature.

'Reaching in'

Outreach, however, involves far more than working in a community setting. It is a much wider process:

It is about access, participation and achievements as a total concept. Any point in that cycle could be out in the community. Most people see this bit (out in the community) as the starting point but it could be at any point in the cycle. (FE inspector)

As observed by Brookfield (1983), there is a common tendency in educational outreach to concentrate on provision of programmes and to neglect the all-important dimension of process. The establishment of community-based programmes of courses, classes and activities tends to become an end in itself, rather than 'the first stage in an evolutionary process which takes the community towards self-actualisation' (p79)

Connections with mainstream

Moreover outreach learning provision may be of limited value if it is a single, one-off, out-based exercise conducted without connection to the main work of a provider. If outreach strategies are totally disconnected from mainstream, they are likely to remain marginal. This is more likely to be the case for some sectors than others (for example pre-92 universities), as two higher education informants suggested:

If you bring them in what do you bring them in to? Here it would be accredited work and a lot of students may not yet be at that intellectual level.

I have pushed and pushed for non-accredited pathways into Level 1. Before they were accrediting everything that walked. There was no coherence. There's still a real parochial feel with most of the academics. We have said there has to be proper collaboration between departments so that people can progress. Some departments are slowly thinking that they need to do something though some of the subject specialists here remain relatively unconvinced.

Some further education informants have found that central funding regimes do not encourage institutions to promote transition from outreach programmes into the main institution:

FEFC inspectors don't really like it if you've got a lot of older adults; it's the skills agenda.

Current funding values colleges with high achievement rates. Some colleges don't want non traditional students because they think they'll drop down the league tables.

Some providers nevertheless take pains to ensure that their outreach work acts as a stepping stone to other opportunities. At Northern College for example, where outreach has always been a central concept: 'it was never an end in itself: it was about inreach. You'd go out and work with organisations but at the back of your mind was bringing groups into the college at an appropriate time.' Here, as in other institutions that cater largely for adult learners, progression routes have been constructed to enable a smooth transition between community and college, and from one level of study to another. Such routes are articulated with mainstream programmes through modules or credits which have a design-fit with mainstream programmes.

Adapting institutions to new student groups

The evidence collected for this study indicates that many further and higher education institutions put all their efforts into the pre-institutional stage and do not use the lessons from successful outreach activities to inform their mainstream procedures and practices. Informants from all sectors felt strongly that this dimension of outreach has been neglected to the detriment of both learners and providers. Some argued that, unless institutional cultures and practices change, many learners who move from community-based into mainstream programmes will withdraw or fail to achieve:

If a major role of institutional outreach is to attract new learners in, then logic suggests that the 'in' bit needs attention. (FE outreach worker)

Outreach isn't just out but in. We need to change the system within universities to keep new kinds of student. Some universities don't know how to get new groups through the doors. Others have done outreach work well but their real problem is transforming the system to keep the students they get. The reception areas of universities are appalling. Some don't have a main entrance, and you meet students wandering about looking for an entrance and prospectuses. No-one knows the rules when they arrive. No maps, no timetables, no access to libraries. This is very difficult for mature students. (HE project officer)

We used to try and shoehorn students into courses but the concept of inclusive learning turned that on its head. What is wrong is the intransigent and inflexible structure. Students don't need to change; it's the structure and the system that need to change and fit around the students. A better match of learning and learners leads to retention and meeting of targets. A key concept then is one of match. If there is a good match people will stay and learn. (FE inspector)

We can bring disaffected people into the college. I can do that, but I can't keep them here. It's not a question of access it's a question of retention – what the college is doing to change its culture and accommodate them. What are we doing internally? New Deal people are like fish out of water. There is an expectation that these students will fit into FE and that there is a nice linear link. This is rubbish! If a person comes in and has a bad experience, he'll never come back.

That's the negative implication of the social inclusion agenda, It's better to do nothing than to do it badly. (FE manager)

These comments suggest that the implications of using outreach as an aid to recruitment have not always been fully grasped in some education institutions and there is still a significant mismatch between community-based and institution-based work.

Another mismatch relates to the costs of learning. Much outreach learning activity, being targeted at 'disadvantaged' groups, is free or low cost but, depending on the programme of study, institutions may require a charge from those who progress into mainstream. Even if this is a small sum it may represent a significant deterrent for some groups of people. In one instance encountered during the course of this study, outreach students on low incomes were being drafted into mainstream college programmes only to find that they had to pay a registration fee:

Students have to be enrolled as college students to get FEFC funding. They then have to pay a £25 college registration fee for one year irrespective of what they're doing. This is an enormous barrier In some circumstances it is possible to waive the fee but it is very awkward.

Moreover, as with the pre-entry process, there can be conflicts of values between staff about the role and purpose of bringing former outreach learners into an institution, as the comments of one informant illustrate:

We had a furious debate about accrediting part-time programmes: arguments about students who went on to university and gained qualifications being seen as betraying the liberal arts tradition. The expectation was that working-class students would go back to their communities. That they would leave with a special free-standing qualification not tainted by the bourgeois education machine. There was some debate among people with a whole string of qualifications themselves about whether we should obstruct progression [to universities].

*   *   *

This chapter has highlighted some of the complexities involved in conducting outreach activities and, by implication, the wide range of skills demanded of the workers who have to deal with these issues on the ground. These will be examined in the next chapter.

CHAPTER FOUR

Outreach staff

As Chapter 3 has illustrated, outreach is by no means a simple and straightforward process and the complexity of the issues involved indicates that employing the right people with the right attributes and blend of skills is probably the most important factor in any community-based work. These may have little to do with qualifications and more to do with personal characteristics as the effectiveness of any outreach endeavour depends ultimately on the web of relationships workers are able to establish in the community. This has obvious implications for staff recruitment:

> *The personal qualities of the outreach worker(s) are seen as being as important as educational qualifications; particularly the ability to make contact and liaise with agencies, community groups, individuals etc.* (Charnley and Withnall, 1989: 43)

> *It is because outreach can be such an unusual job that special consideration needs to be given by those engaged in recruitment and those considering applying for outreach posts....Formal qualifications whilst obviously valuable are not critical when it comes to this kind of work. Much more important is the candidate's personality and presence in the company of strangers. In other words, their interpersonal skills. These skills are learnt in everyday life and not on personal development courses. It is much easier to recruit someone who is very happy dealing with people from all walks of life and train them, for example, to write reports than it is to take a well-qualified recluse and train them (sic) to get on with people. The personality of the potential outreach worker is critical to the success of the outreach endeavour.* (Gilman, 1992: 10)

Not everyone can (or should) do outreach. Work on widening participation consistently shows that those who take on the job of contacting people who historically do not take advantage of organised learning opportunities are more likely to be accepted when they have backgrounds and characteristics similar to those of the groups targeted. People of the same gender and ethnic group, who speak the same language or have the same accent, and who have already established local credibility, are more likely to be trusted than those who do not have any characteristics in common with the communities contacted.

Any analysis of the tasks and challenges involved in outreach will reveal the extraordinarily wide range of skills it demands.

Outreach skill needs

The literature shows that outreach work can be divided into a number of key stages:

- identification of target areas and groups
- local research
- establishing relationships with other providers and relevant agencies working in the same areas and with the same groups
- making face-to-face contact with people in the target groups and communities and engaging them in a process of identifying their learning interests and needs
- negotiating learning activities with target groups
- supporting them through the learning process.

To work through these stages outreach workers require a combination of practical and interpersonal skills. The evidence from the literature and practitioners shows that at the pre-programme stage, these include the ability to:

- conduct local research and analyse data
- identify key local networks and individuals
- communicate and negotiate effectively with a variety of people at different levels and establish relationships based on mutual trust
- organise meetings with disparate groups and agencies
- engage people, as individuals or in groups, in dialogue about their interests and priorities
- identify and understand learning interests and needs and devise appropriate ways of meeting them
- secure the necessary support and resources to set up responsive activities
- develop partnerships with local agencies and other providers to facilitate outreach arrangements
- work in a way that does not impose institutional values and bias
- work outside traditional funding models
- work autonomously and sometimes in isolation
- handle conflict.

At the programme delivery stage, outreach workers need the ability to:

- organise and administer programmes in response to identified interests
- help groups to identify programme aims and objectives without imposing own preferences and values

- facilitate activities without controlling them
- help people to identify their existing knowledge, skills and talents
- establish mechanisms for progression routes and referrals to other providers
- find resources to provide any forms of support that are required (such as transport, costs, childcare)
- evaluate progress and outcomes
- produce written reports.
  (Johnston, 1968; REPLAN, 1988; Watson and Tyers, 1998; Wood, 2000)

In performing all of these tasks, outreach workers need to have:

- sensitivity
- respect for others and host communities:
  Outreach workers must have a fundamental respect for local people's views, experiences and potential, and see their own role as that of a facilitator rather than as a controller of resources and/or expertise. (REPLAN Review No. 1, DES, 1986.)
- flexibility: the ability to adapt to different situations; to adopt different approaches with different groups and to react to widely differing wants and needs. A lesson that emerged from the DfEE demonstration projects was that outreach workers should be prepared to change the way they work in response to different situations and different groups: 'Approaches have been used, repeated or discarded as the immediate situation demands.' (Clarke and Taubman, 1981, 55). Both Gilman (1992) and MacSween (1993) comment that different approaches are required for contacting and working with men and women.
- the ability to identify and call on other sources of skill and expertise:
  There are benefits from using a team approach in outreach schemes so that there can be a mix of skills and experience and the opportunity for mutual support. Workers may find they have to adopt other roles – counsellor, confidante, 'social worker' – in the course of their work. (Charnley and Withnall, 1989: 43)

It is unrealistic that any one person…could hope to acquire the range of professional skills necessary to lead a group through its stages of development, because he or she would need to be a legal adviser, counsellor, personnel officer, press officer, etc. Thus his [sic] task, together with his colleagues, is to provide some of these skills, secure help from other professionals and agencies to supply others and above all train people in them. The major skills for the work {are} interpersonal and organisational, with sufficient political competence to make the most of the system to get resources. (Portwood, 1988: 17)

Making the right contacts

The crucial stage of outreach is, of course, reaching and contacting target groups. Outreach workers usually operate through a mixture of 'cold' contacts – door-knocking, handing out leaflets, approaching people in the street, at school gates, etc. – or 'snowballing' contacts: following up leads and contacts provided by others. According to Gilman (1992: 39) many outreach workers prefer the latter as many people dislike being accosted by strangers:

> *Think about the times that you have been approached by complete strangers. Who were they? What did they want? How did you react? One outreach worker was attempting to make cold contacts with a group of young people who, unknown to the worker, were regularly harassed by a religious tout. For these young people being approached by strangers carrying rucksacks meant one thing only – loony!*

To find out about a specific area or community, outreach workers need to identify the main communication channels and the 'key' people: those with a high profile who are known and respected in a neighbourhood, and familiar with local issues. This involves spending time in an area, observing, interacting with and listening to residents to get a feel for local networks:

> *In the village where I live – population 400…we have to understand the numerous overlapping and interlocking conduits which operate – the two church congregations; the two pub regulars, the newcomers; the 'born and bred there community'; the footballers, cricketers, gardeners, horse lovers, dog walkers, and last but not least the school-gate brigade. All this complements the written communication through church magazines, parish council news-sheets, occasional free newspapers and what is stapled to telegraph posts* (Soulsby, 1999: 9)

As some have noted (Watson and Tyers, 1998), the 'chemistry' of local areas varies greatly. In some areas, the church may have a higher profile in community matters than other local organisations or institutions (one person interviewed for this study reported that in a nearby village 'the vicar attracts money like a magnet'); in other areas it is the local school or post-office. An outreach guide produced a decade ago for the REPLAN Programme suggests that there is no single formula for success in making contact with community networks and local leaders/activists, and it is possible for outreach workers to waste time cultivating the wrong people or inappropriate groups.

> *The secret lies in identifying individuals, groups and organisations:*
>
> ● *who have the capacity to communicate with a wide range of other people and organisations through whom local energy is effectively channelled*
> ● *who have the ability to develop and maintain adequate arrangements for*

the support and nurturing of collective effort
- *who are well-regarded by the target audience and organisations with which you are particularly concerned.* (FEU/REPLAN, 1990b: 20)

According to Watson and Tyers (1998), working with organisations or people who already have a high profile and positive image helps to establish their credibility and reduces lead time. Their local knowledge can also help workers to avoid mistakes. In one of the outreach demonstration projects, workers intended to use inserts in the local free press to ensure that all local residents received information about the initiative. However, it emerged that residents on a particular estate did not have access to the newspapers as no one would deliver them owing to the reputation of the area. Other means of distribution consequently had to be found.

A common pitfall is to become overly associated with a particular group which can lead to rejection by others (Smith, 1994). To establish the right contacts therefore involves investment of time and considerable skill, and in some cases contact with targeted groups can only be achieved through an appropriate intermediary:

There are networks in which local educators cannot hope to get a working foothold…Those used to working directly with 'clients' have to move to the idea of working with (or through) intermediaries (Smith, 1994: 116)

Working with community gatekeepers

In widening participation partnership work conducted in Oxfordshire (outlined in McGivney, 2000), development workers succeeded in reaching specific target groups only after negotiation with the 'gatekeepers' such as community and religious leaders, head teachers, health visitors, employers, managers, bail hostel wardens and probation officers. Negotiating with the gatekeepers is one of the most important aspects of outreach as the success of any initiative may depend on their co-operation, commitment and support. This in turn depends on the extent to which they are persuaded of the value of the work both to target groups and to themselves.

Some outreach and development workers find that gaining the co-operation of gatekeepers is far more difficult than persuading non-participants to participate. Efforts to contact particular groups can be seen as encroachments on individual territory and therefore resisted. Some people may be reluctant to co-operate because they do not perceive educational approaches as useful or necessary to the group in question. They may also be over-protective towards the people in their charge or feel threatened by the idea of having better educated individuals working for or with them. Those who do agree to co-operate sometimes have a view of a group's learning interests and needs that is at variance with *actual* interests and needs, and which corresponds more with their own beliefs and attitudes. This can affect the kind of activities they are prepared to facilitate.

To deal with challenges such as these, outreach workers have to display considerable tact, persistence and persuasiveness. They need to enter into an early dialogue with community leaders and other gatekeepers about the nature and purposes of the activities proposed and their potential outcomes. Getting the messages right at this stage is crucial for, in order to give their support, these individuals will need to feel a sense of ownership and be persuaded that they have more to gain than to lose. Like any other group the gatekeepers have diverse characteristics, values, pressures and priorities; therefore any approaches to them need to be just as sensitive as approaches to the groups providers are trying to reach.

Having made the right contacts, outreach workers then need to enter into genuine engagement with the target communities:

> *They are there not simply to learn about the area but to intervene, To do this effectively…entails…gaining an active appreciation of local networks and relationships, of how things work, of the norms and values of different groups within the area; of power relations and 'important' people.*
>
> *[They] must gain a knowledge of life within the area and how such local knowledge relates to the world beyond. In a very real sense they have to become 'part of the local community'; to participate in local ways of life; to engage in a living relationship with people and with place.* (Smith, 1994: pp. 15 and 19)

> *Engaging with different experience must mean participating with that experience, 'being there' – sitting on management committees, organising and joining in community events, helping at the local crèche – and not just working with a group to set up a course. Real engagement works both ways and should change educators' institutions, practices and ideas.* (Stuart and Thomson, 1995: 10)

The evidence shows that the outreach worker's contribution to the effectiveness of any locally-based initiative cannot be underestimated. This is illustrated in the list of the factors identified as accounting for the success of one of the Adult and Community Learning Fund projects – CREATE (Creating Equality of Access to Training and Employment) at the Five Lamps Organisation in Thornaby, Stockton on Tees – a project providing targeted provision in particular curriculum areas and in local venues:

- the key outreach worker's local knowledge, his credibility amongst residents and his unbounded enthusiasm for learning and faith in its value
- the thoroughness of the outreach worker's approach which includes careful follow-up of all enquiries and expressions of interest and willingness to keep returning if he had called at an inconvenient time
- his commitment, thoroughness, and willingness to start where people are without preconceptions; his patience and preparedness to draw people bit by bit; his belief in what people can achieve with support

- good networking and partnerships with key people, local organisations and education partners
- quick responses to any expressions of interest in learning either by supporting people into learning programmes or arranging programmes for groups. This means there is less time for interest to fade or further obstacles to interfere with participation
- incorporating small group, bite-sized learning provision as part of the strategy and following through with careful information and guidance to draw people into further provision
- willingness within the project to allow time (and budgets) for outreach to develop and to see success in realistic terms, particularly in relationship to numbers enrolling on courses in the initial phases. (Information supplied by Cheryl Turner, NIACE)

Challenges

Although outreach work can be personally very rewarding, many workers routinely experience a number of challenges. The major ones identified during the course of this study were:

- Combating community resistance and distrust of education institutions.
- Being fair (and seen to be fair) in allocations of resources and dealings with different groups even when they have conflicting views and needs.
- Working within inflexible funding regimes:
  One of the most difficult things has been getting my head round working with external funding and being led by 'outcomes'. You need to make sure that outcomes are the things you want to do. We have to be pragmatic because we know we have to stay within budget. (FE outreach worker)
- Isolation and working entirely on one's own.
- Insufficient recognition, by managers and funders, of how much time it takes before results may be seen.
- Persuading institutional managers to recognise outcomes other than increasing recruitment and financial benefits for the institution
- Lack of institutional support.
- Conflicts between personal and institutional values. As indicated earlier, one of the biggest problems is when the desire to help people is incompatible with the structures, constraints and interests of the employing provider. Many outreach workers are caught between two worlds – those of the professionals for whom they work and those of the people with whom they work. As Gilman (1992: 11) observes, they have to combine an understanding of the two and, 'in straddling these two "worlds", they have to deal with a whole series of ambivalent situations'. This can lead to conflicts in loyalties that may cause considerable stress:

[Outreach workers] have largely taken the tension between the structures they have to work in and people's real demands into themselves, constantly 'bending, squeezing and fiddling' and the resulting stress has been damaging to the workers, and prevented dialogue between the people who controlled resources and those who wanted them. (Nicholls and Murray, 1981: 57)

Despite these problems, many workers find outreach work very worthwhile and experience what Brookfield (1983: 200) has described as 'the intense satisfaction of receiving genuine testimony to the effects such work can have on individuals' lives'. The mixture of satisfactions and challenges it generates for workers have been described in a REPLAN publication (1989):

The attractions of working outside an institution are many. Some people find the freedom this allows to be refreshing and challenging, enabling the development of a whole range of individual skills. There is also the opportunity to be part of real change and growth. Work is undertaken with people on their own terms rather than on the terms of the institution alone. Working in the community can also be frustrating, time consuming and depressing, yet with proper support, supervision and evaluation it is more likely to be challenging and satisfying with a degree of freedom which is found in few other areas of education. It can also bring a new dimension and dynamism to institutions in these times of rapid change.

The dedication and commitment of those encountered during the course of this study were never in doubt:

I never leave a new contact without having a name, address and telephone number. The key is patience: so many people I've come across have had a raw deal from education. (Senior outreach worker)

One college manger attributed the success of outreach work in one estate to the fact that the outreach worker 'has been there 24 hours a day, 7 days a week for the last 18 months'.

Staff recruitment

The personal qualities and skills required in doing this kind of work are therefore multiple. As an outreach team leader commented:

The more I look at it the more skills I see it needs: negotiating; relation to people at different levels; work across the spectrum, very high inter-personal skills, Not everyone can do it. As someone said 'you have to be like an octopus! (LEA outreach worker)

Outreach workers need passion and commitment and interpersonal skills to make things happen on the ground. They need to engage in meaningful discourse at the professional level but also with people on the ground. They must switch register without being patronising. I suspect that it is quite rare being able to bring these two levels into creative engagement. We were looking for staff who were hybrids. (Former college manager)

Some people interviewed for the study felt that the skills and qualities required in educational outreach work are not always appreciated by funders and institutional managers. Some observed that many people with the right skills and experience have left the sector and are being replaced by individuals unsuited to this kind of work. According to an LEA officer:

The real problem is that outreach and development skills are soft skills which are not recognised and providers think anyone can do it. There's a dearth of good people. Younger people aren't coming through plus there's competition from other sectors such as community development and health.

It is probably in the voluntary and community sector that people with the skills and experience can still be found. A recent study revealed that many WEA staff have these and the expertise required to fulfil the multiple roles outlined earlier in this chapter:

WEA staff have particular skills in outreach work and developing local networks. These are essential WEA skills. Staff necessarily spend a lot of their time working out in the community alone. Unless they are trusted, respected and widely known throughout the local community they cannot perform effectively as WEA staff.

Staff possess the ability to spot opportunities (including niches in the local learning market) and explore and discuss these with other community bodies. This necessitates listening, identifying local needs, determining what funding and other resources might be available, which organisations are best able to contribute and where additional resources might be obtained, deciding what the WEA can best contribute and deciding what partnership models are most suitable to met the defined needs, and which roles can most suitable be played by each of the partners.

Staff know how to target learning to match the learning needs of local communities and particular groups within those communities. They can be particularly successful in ensuring that education programmes are correctly targeted and that local communities and special groups obtain dedicated support. [They] are highly experienced in developing local grassroots community partnerships, at helping these develop and expand so that they create new networks and partnerships. [They] are flexible – willing to find ways of responding to a wide variety of local needs and target groups and to innovate;... skilled and experienced in raising short-term finance for learning. (Ford and Jackson, 1999: 4, 10)

Most of the outreach workers in the institutions and organisations contacted for the study were women. Sometimes this was attributed to the fact that women are good at interpersonal and communications skills; sometimes to the fact that outreach posts are often insecure part-time or temporary positions and therefore do not attract men:

> *Male outreach workers are difficult to come by. All our dealings tend to be with women practitioners. Women see outreach in terms of empowering others. We know that in terms of numbers, in nine times out of ten, outreach efforts will fail but because of women's commitment, they'll keep trying. Male development officers fall at the first hurdle. I have drawn a complete blank on men.*

The same gender gap has also been noticed in the recruitment of volunteers to act as learning champions:

> *When volunteers were found, they have tended to be recent learners and female… It has been far more problematic to find male volunteers, especially when male 'champions for learning' have been sought.* (Watson and Tyers, 1998: 231)

Professional standing and status

In contrast to the range of skills demanded of them, and the multiple and sensitive tasks they are expected to perform, many education outreach staff are in low status and often short-term positions. This has traditionally been the case: one worker referred to outreach as having always been 'a non-job' or an 'apology job' despite its importance. Another reported that her college principal refused to accept that outreach activities were 'work'. Although this study found examples of organisations where outreach staff enjoy good and secure conditions of service, in the majority, the people engaged to do development work were appointed on a part-time and short-term basis, usually on a year-on-year budget basis or for the duration of funding for a project or initiative. Even in the WEA, according to one informant:

> *Funding the groundwork is difficult: there's no money for outreach workers. They tend to be short-term funded despite their being the most important link in the chain.*

This puts outreach workers in a difficult position. Several consulted during this study said that they felt insecure and marginalised in relation to institution-based staff, and some reported tension with their colleagues, especially if they tried to change systems to accommodate new groups of learners.

> *Teaching staff don't like outreach much because it's very threatening. You're disturbing the idea of 'teachers' and 'classes' Some people see outreach work as the job of people with gaps in their timetable.*

I was seen as an evil woman after I made changes in the entrant interviews system.

Tension between outreach and institution-based staff is alluded to frequently in the literature:

There are examples where...the outreach worker has been marginalised by other workers on the grounds that outreach work is 'not a real profession'. (Gilman, 1992: 45)

Outreach workers {in ILEA} have been...often isolated, sometimes shunned within Institutes. [They] were of a comparatively low formal status within their Institutes...Their work was mysterious and often troublesome to the smooth running of the Institute....every change in procedure had to be fought for; most actions were mistrusted. (Clarke and Taubman, 1981: 551; Taubman and Cushman, 1981: 43 and 45)

Isolation, lack of support and training, low status...many outreach workers would support these criticisms of their job. (REPLAN, 1986: 8)

There often exists an institutional indifference to the effort of educators. The battles which educators and community workers have to fight to maintain resources and secure institutional recognition leave scars which take the form of a sense of professional marginality and isolation. (Brookfield, 1983: 201)

The evidence gathered for this study indicated that the low and temporary status of many outreach workers have negative consequences:

- The work itself may be perceived as low status:
- 'Short-term budgets and temporary staffing usually signal low priority work. Furthermore staff can be limited by the project timescales and priorities'. (McNair, 1999: 31)
- They can lead to reduced worker energy and commitment:
  It's not easy if you're on a temporary contract to put your heart and soul into a community and there's early burn out because of the intensity of support that's required (College outreach worker quoted in McGivney, 1999: 91)
- They lead to high staff turnover causing disruption and lack of continuity:
  Several co-ordinators were appointed on a part-time basis. This nearly always brought challenges of conflicting priorities and pressures. Part-time post-holders have also been more likely to leave part way during a project.
  Where posts are both part-time and temporary, staff turnover will inevitably be high. In projects of this type, gaps (as post-holders leave) and periods of induction and 'picking up the ropes' can be a major distraction. (Watson and Tyers, 1998: 2.09)
- The work does not have any impact on the provider's overall procedures and practices:

In most cases 'outreach' experiments remained just that, experiments. The main body of the AEI's work and ILEA's bureaucratic procedures rolled on untouched. (Taubman and Cushman, 1981: 44)

Short-term project staff, sometimes located on the margins of the institution, and with relatively little status in institutional hierarchies, may not be well placed to see the possibilities of institutional change, or exert leverage over it, and this was a notable problem in the first years of some [NABCE] projects. Most of the eight projects reporting high importance and high success in producing institutional change were unusual in the seniority of their project leaders, and in the extent to which the work was embedded in broader institutional development strategies in place before the project began. (McNair, 1999: 31)

Conversely, better conditions of service have generally been found to lead to greater effectiveness:

It has been found that where outreach workers have been employed continually it has been much more effective in getting people in. (County outreach team co-ordinator)

Outreach workers can be much more effective if they are part of a team, either within an agency or by establishing their own team structure by joint working with other professionals. It is, however, primarily the responsibility of managers, administrators or organisers to ensure that outreach workers are given adequate support, status and resources. (REPLAN, 1986: 8)

While a major reason for outreach workers' sometimes marginal status is often determined by the short-term budgets available for this kind of work, Brookfield (1983: 200-201) identified another reason for their ambiguous position within providing organisations, namely, the fundamental incompatibility between an institution's need to provide courses and attract new learners to them, and the outreach worker's wish to work with community groups in ways that may not generate new learners for a provider. Brookfield also observed that the status and visibility of outreach workers tend to rise or decline in direct proportion to the length and intensity of outside scrutiny of an organisation's student profile:

Ambiguity will probably be manifest in the institutional attitude adopted towards those who choose to work in an informal mode with groups and individuals. The raison d'etre of most AE programmes tends to be the increase of student numbers through ever more plentiful courses and classes. Anyone who challenges this rationale runs a professional risk of being denied the opportunity to climb the ladder of institutional reward bestowed in the form of job promotion or increased funding. On the other hand, it may sometimes serve an institution's needs very conveniently to be able to wheel out a token informal or outreach worker whose clients will be from groups proportionately under-represented in the general student clientele. Most adult education programmers will know of individuals who work with community groups in an informal mode and who occupy the lowest position on the institutional ladder of job prestige and institutional resources. However, when those same institutions are attacked for the elitist nature of their provision, then the outreach worker suddenly becomes the object of institutional approval. This shift in the focus of institutional attention often lasts no longer than the period of political concentration or external criticism of the rigidity or elitism of the institution's programme. Once this threat is removed, the educator then becomes assigned to that peculiar professional limbo so familiar to (though not beloved of) community workers, outreach workers and informal educators of all kinds.

While these observations may be considered a trifle cynical, the evidence suggests that they still have a strong element of truth.

Given the centrality of outreach to current widening participation and social inclusion agendas, it is clearly important to appoint outreach workers, so far as possible, on terms that are sufficiently favourable to allow them to perform the multiple and sensitive tasks outlined earlier:

> *The status and role of outreach workers, {is} a vital matter. A national survey of...projects...revealed that the most favourable terms and conditions for this kind of worker were usually achieved through secondment policies rather than by special appointments. This gives workers a sense of security and offers the best opportunity for the work to become mainstream.* (Portwood, 1988: 20)

Managerial support of managers is another key to the effectiveness of any outreach endeavour. In some examples outlined in Chapter 2, the support and commitment of managerial champions was considered to be one of the most critical success factors. Managerial support can take a number of forms:

- recognition that outreach is an integral part of an institution's work, not automatically low level or second best
- the setting of realistic and achievable aims and targets
- allocation of appropriate resources and provision of adequate infrastructure support (office accommodation, administrative and clerical support, telephone)
- recognition that effective work in the community requires time and flexibility and allowing for this in work schedules
- discussion with outreach workers about how to make the most effective response to identified interests and needs
- provision of adequate supervision and mechanisms for regular analysis and evaluation of the work
- provision of support to help workers address the kind of problems that arise in outreach work

- ensuring that institution-based staff understand the role of outreach workers and that outreach staff are integrated with and see themselves as part of the whole staff team. In this respect, the Oxfordshire County Council strategy to ensure that outreach workers meet and interact on a regular basis with other key adult education staff could be emulated
- provision of in-service training opportunities for outreach staff especially if they are on short-term contracts, including opportunities to gain appropriate qualifications.

Staff development

Effective community-based provision demands a range of skills on the part of providers. These include negotiation, facilitation, appropriate teaching and learning styles, guidance, networking, development planning and financial management. While some practitioners have developed expertise in many of these areas, others have had minimal support. All staff engaged in such provision need to upgrade their skills and to learn from the expertise of colleagues from other sectors. (Scottish Office, 1996: 33)

Given the range of skills required in outreach work, many feel that staff development should be a priority. Not everyone will have the right blend of skills and this underlines the need for training not only for development workers but for tutors who are not used to working with new groups of students or working in non institutional settings. Appropriate training could also help managers and institution-based staff to benefit from the knowledge and expertise of outreach staff in order to better support the progression of new groups from community settings into an educational environment. Some of the staff interviewed for this study have found that teaching staff are currently struggling with the widening participation agenda:

A problem is expecting our staff to go and teach on a range of locations. They aren't confident enough to do that, Delivering at a local level is very valuable and they benefit from it but it's hard to do if they haven't done it before. (FE manager)

Staff need to be trained to deal with the disaffected. PGCEs don't teach you that. It's a false expectation to expect FE lecturers at the front line to be able to deal with new groups. How can you expect our staff to deal with users who have never walked through the door? You'll never achieve inclusion just from the bottom up. There has to be top-down bottom-up synergy. Unfortunately those at the top don't realise they have to change. I think all staff should have skills training on dealing with the disaffected, The sector needs tools for doing the job. Are we really taking on their needs? (FE manager)

Training local people

An increasing dimension of educational outreach is the recruitment of local people who have local contacts and credibility within different communities, and training them to be learning champions or 'signposters', and to take the work further when projects come to an end. Training local workers was a feature of several of the DfEE demonstration outreach projects, and variously entailed on-the-job training, training programmes with OCN accreditation and referral to other project strands involving training (Watson and Tyers, 1998). Some problems were nevertheless encountered. In one instance a local worker was unable to gain a qualification in guidance from the local college because of inability to meet the fees. Moreover, when projects tried to provide some form of payment, there were sometimes difficulties over entitlement to and potential loss of benefits:

> *One of the barriers to generating volunteers from the community has been concerns over the loss of benefits. Even where projects have agreed to pay their volunteers an hourly rate, there have been difficulties in making these payments without affecting benefits. Ways round this have included phasing of payments, and deeming payments to be 'incentives for participation' rather than wages. Informal liaison with local staff of the Benefits Agency has also helped.* (Watson and Tyers, 1998: 230)

The demonstration projects suggested that in order to perform this kind of role effectively it is necessary for workers to come off benefits or to have other part-time work in order to receive the hourly rate.

* * *

This chapter has suggested that the effectiveness of any outreach initiative depends ultimately on the skills and personality of the workers concerned, the terms and conditions of their appointment, and the extent of management support, supervision and training they receive. The wide range of skills involved in outreach and their relevance to social inclusion and widening participation suggests that there is an urgent need to develop an accredited national training programme that will help people acquire the core skills to perform this important work.

The effectiveness of outreach also depends on the resources made available for it. While the success of any approach relies heavily on the skills of outreach workers, they themselves have to operate within the constraints of specific project funding or budget allocations and this may severely limit the extent and impact of their activities.

CHAPTER FIVE

Funding outreach

The extent, nature and status of outreach activities depend to a large extent on the way they are funded. Since outreach is now inextricably connected with the notion of disadvantage it is inevitably – as all outreach workers will tell you – time-consuming and expensive. However, as they will also tell you, it is also the most effective way of engaging with the large number of people who do not take advantage of organised adult learning opportunities:

It's very expensive but unless that work is done we know we're not going to reach the non participants. There are levels of non participation and some groups will never be reached without this kind of work. (FE manager)

It's very expensive but it's placing value on the most deprived groups in our society. (HE project officer)

We all know how hard, time consuming and expensive it is to get people in. You may work with 60 but only get 10 in. (FE inspector)

Although widening participation is considered an increasingly important role of all post 16 education institutions, there is no single funding mechanism for outreach and development work with adults. As outlined in previous chapters, however, a number of initiatives and sources of funding have fostered the development or expansion of outreach activity targeted at communities identified as disadvantaged and excluded. The Single Regeneration Budget (SRB), the Adult and Community Learning Fund (ACLF), the FEFC Non-Schedule 2 pilots, the New Opportunities Fund and various programmes within the European structural funds, are all being used to support strategies to widen participation and encourage community regeneration. These funding sources are generally considered more flexible than mainstream post-16 funding streams. For the outreach project at South Trafford College, for example (see Chapter 2), a 'critical success factor' was identified as the flexibility of ACLF funding: 'ACLF funding made things happen in contrast to other funding with all their paperwork and bureaucracy. We couldn't have done it within the funding constraints of the college.'

However, colleges which are currently funded on student entry, progression and exit can, for the first stage, use the resource at their own discretion and put any surpluses into the pre-entry stage, even as a loss leader. The postcode factor also favours outreach development and the special funds for widening participation and partnerships have generated a number of innovative approaches. However, the latter have entailed a competitive bidding process and have generally been short-term. The work has consequently often remained marginal and has not had much impact on the system.

In Higher Education, the HEFCE Non Award-Bearing Continuing Education programme (NABCE) enabled a number of institutions to develop innovative provision in their local communities. Subsequent mainstream formula funding for widening provision has included monitoring of participation by postcodes. HEFCE now also offers funding premiums to higher education institutions that recruit and retain students from under-represented groups. Since October 1999, all English higher education institutions (HEIs) have been required to produce strategic statements and plans relating to widening participation as part of their corporate strategy. Strategies are expected to include admission and retention targets with regard to under-represented groups in the sector and these will be monitored on an annual basis and linked to the provision of widening participation funding. Special funding has also been allocated for building partnerships between HEIs and other institutions and organisations for meeting local or regional needs and promoting longer-term commitment to widening participation. A HEFCE document refers to the:

> *key aim to increase the recruitment and retention of students from under-represented groups, primarily through formula funding but also through a complementary special funding programme to support partnerships, innovation and development work* (HEFCE, 1999: 1)

Among the areas where institutions are expected to be active and incur additional costs are special recruitment schemes including outreach and summer schools.

Despite the availability of new sources of funding and the shifts in mainstream funding to encourage the participation of new segments of the population, many practitioners consider the whole area of community-based work to be still under-resourced. During the course of this study, informants from the further and higher education sectors frequently referred to the limited nature of funding support available for networking and development work:

> *Funding for community work is minimal. Leverage from funding is really too limited to tip the balance. It's usually limited to appointing people like me. In terms of HE, outreach continues to be marginal and always has to have special funding that is time-limited. Formula funding will always be about student support, retention and things like compacts.* (HE project officer)

There's a tension between the way we fund courses (e.g. through FEFC) and some outreach practice. If you empower people in the community, there may be no finance in that for the institution. That's why our energies are directed towards courses that generate income. The thrust is towards bringing people towards traditional AE. There must be a way around that but it will take a long time to move away from that system. (FE manager)

Since outreach work is often funded on a short-term project basis (except in those institutions where it is an integral part of mainstream activity), it is frequently considered to be of low status and value. It can consequently be difficult to continue the work or to embed it in institutional arrangements at the end of the funding term. It has been suggested (Kinneavy, 1988) that a three-year cycle of funding support is the minimum period necessary for effective community development work. However, even after this period it it may disappear. The evaluation of the Non-Award Bearing Continuing Education (NABCE) programme in higher education found that while the availability of ring-fenced funding over four years had enabled institutions to engage in innovative development work which they would otherwise not have been able to do, some of it would inevitably disappear at the end of the funding term due to: 'other more powerful institutional and cultural pressures' (McNair, 1999: 8).

In his study of institutional outreach (tellingly sub-titled 'Ragged round the Edges'), Stewart (1995) described the relationship between institutions and their outreach work as ambivalent: he found the work was generally poorly resourced; not embedded in institutional structures and widely perceived to be marginalised. Five years on, although new funding sources are encouraging an increase in community-based work, whether there is a genuine commitment to it is open to question. Inevitably the availability of funding will encourage organisations to make proposals that fit the criteria irrespective of whether they have the necessary experience or interest in working in this way. As McNair (1999: 63) observed in relation to the NABCE programme in higher education:

While institutions acted in good faith in their use of NABCE funding, it is clear that the level of real commitment to the work does not always match the formal mission statements.

A similar point has been made by Fremeaux (2000: 66):

Funding tends to shape the conceptualisation of (community) projects. Crudely speaking, if...money is in regeneration, attributed to projects facilitating capacity-building in communities, organisations are going to conceive their projects along those lines. Whether it reveals a genuine interest in these sort of schemes, a true concern and real attempt to benefit the community, or a strategy to get the money...is currently an embarrassing question.

Some providers and outreach workers who reported to this study resent the fact that funding for this work often requires them to collude in a bidding culture based on specific areas and groups identified as 'disadvantaged'. Some have also become frustrated with having to spend valuable time bidding for very small amounts of money that, according to one, has 'to be sorted out in 5 minutes by the end of the financial year'. The problem of temporary funding impinges particularly on the voluntary sector and negatively affects their ability to deliver effective learning and regeneration activities which will have a lasting impact on the communities they serve. According to one practitioner who has worked in several different sectors, it is common for outreach projects to disappear at the end of the funding term, only to be 'revamped' when the next bit of 'fashionable' funding comes along.

Investment of time

The problem most commonly identified with short-term funding for outreach work is that it does not take account of the demanding nature of the processes involved or recognise how long it can be before tangible results will be visible. The first stage of outreach – establishing links in the community – is often the most time-consuming stage. As the ESOL network co-ordinator at North East London College has found: 'This kind of work takes an awful lot of time. It could have taken me a whole week just contacting one or two organisations.' Similarly, an account of a project set up to establish links between a college and local communities described the amount of time taken up by visits and local networking activities as exacting but essential to establish the college within the local community (Kinneavy, 1989: 69). Accordingly, a key lesson from the DfEE demonstration projects was never to underestimate the time it takes to organise and implement outreach initiatives, as the lead times invariably tend to be longer than anticipated (Watson and Tyers, 1998). This message is still not fully understood at some levels of policy and institutional management:

You've got to spend time on the pre-figurative stuff in the community; talking to people. But no-one sees this as real work. It's too loose and unstructured, but you can't reach these people any other way.

The important thing is the first hook. Once you've got them through the door the possibilities are endless. It's the investment in that stage which is the most important.

You could say the battle's won once you've got them through the door. It's the previous nine months that are the really hard work. Outreach work needs to be done in the pub and that often means in the evening. You need staff and resources to do this. (Community development workers quoted in McGivney, 1999: 91)

The short-term nature of many of the sources of support available for development work can undermine the very objectives for which they were established – to encourage change and regeneration within deprived areas and groups. This built-in contradiction has been highlighted by Fremeaux (2000: 66):

> *If long-term projects are not encouraged more strongly how can long-term benefits be expected from the community it {funding} addresses? These schemes tend to be highly restricted by the year to year current system of funding which hinders long-term planning and long-term implementation. The community ends up being engaged with one-off events which, before they have had the time to have affected the community in-depth, are already over.*

Moreover, as several outreach workers reported to this study, it is often impossible to contact and involve the most deprived and hard-to-reach groups within very short time-scales. Since work with such groups often takes a long period to become established, providers may end up working with more easily contacted sections of the community who may already be catered for, or less in need of special interventions. This clearly defeats the purpose of targeting funding at the 'most disadvantaged'.

> *If funding is very short-scale, the danger is you'll be reaching people who are more accessible and aware.* (FE outreach worker)

> *The whole of the first year, which I spent visiting and explaining, was an uphill struggle making contact. The contacts and recruitment I did in the first year didn't really get the right people. We were getting people who already knew the networks and appreciated what I was doing and were able to get release.* (FE outreach worker)

> *I spend so much of my time trying to make contact with people that often the definition of my {outreach} role stops there* (quoted in Wood, 2000)

On the other hand, the availability of special funding for outreach and development work has a number of advantages: it encourages providers to take risks and experiment with new approaches that they might not otherwise consider; receipt of such funds can give a higher profile and status to this kind of work in an institution, and it can also be a factor in attracting additional funding from other sources. McNair (1999) summarised these benefits in relation to the Non-Award Bearing Continuing Education (NABCE) Programme in higher education, but also stressed the overall marginality of the projects funded by pointing out that even for the largest of them, the funding amounted to less than 1 per cent of the institution's overall HEFCE grant. Despite the fact that most of the NABCE projects 'explored important territory for the future of their institutions and the HE system':

many were not seen by their host institution as having a contribution to make to its the strategic agenda, and some had no route to connect their work to mainstream institutional decision-making. (McNair, 1999: 49)

Nevertheless, some of the largest NABCE projects sought:

to address multiple strategic agendas, and at their best these were closely integrated into institutional mission and strategy, with strong support from senior managers. In many of these, the funding served to accelerate and improve the quality of work already identified as a priority, but undeliverable within existing resources.

This summarises the three key elements necessary to make maximum use of short-term funding: connection with institutional mission, senior managerial support and extension of work already started or considered a priority.

Sustainability

On the whole, however, post-funding sustainability is a real issue for outreach work that is funded on a temporary basis and it raises questions about how outreach workers should manage the cessation of funding. The DfEE-funded demonstration outreach projects (Watson and Tyers, 1998) confirmed that, without a strategy for embedding the work, it will not bear dividends beyond the funding period. Continuation strategies therefore need to be put in place if initiatives are to have any lasting impact and if providers are to maintain community credibility. Portwood (1988: 24) warns outreach workers against leaving an initiative or area too soon and suggests that withdrawal should be gradual to avoid resentment and loss of the trust that has been painstakingly built up. He suggests that groups who feel they have been let down may not be inclined to accept other approaches from education providers in the future.

Some outreach workers have circumvented the problem of short-term funding by finding other sources of financial support. In several of the demonstration projects, for example, new funding for whole or parts of the work was secured from sources such as the European Social Fund and the Single Regeneration Budget. However, in some cases, workers found that there were pitfalls in moving to a less flexible funding regime. One project which was being considered for incorporation into an SRB funding initiative was required to adopt a more target-driven approach which could have led to the people most in need of help missing out:

The likelihood of having to switch from the flexible funding of this initiative to more target-driven funding streams has caused some concerns. Thus far, projects have been able to help a wide variety of people; the concern is that now they may be forced to focus on those who are more job or education 'ready'. (Watson and Tyers, 1998: 241)

Some of the people interviewed for this study reported similar concerns. While the ESOL training courses at North East London College referred to in Chapter 2 could continue after the end of the funding term: 'they would need to be run on an FEFC model which wouldn't be suitable. The trainees need an incredible amount of tutorial support. It would be very difficult to provide this within an FEFC model.'

Seeking out other sources of funding is therefore an important means of sustaining community-based initiatives but it entails the risk of imposing changes on the nature and style of the work. There is a fundamental incompatibility between outreach and development work within different communities and the audit culture operated by most mainstream funding regimes. Moreover, a particular problem associated with formula funding is the stress on student numbers. This is incompatible with the nature of much outreach work which frequently starts with small numbers of learners:

Real local initiatives may start with only two or three people as a maximum, not 13.5. [We] have had to hunt for loopholes to support small groups, and apologise for the small numbers in local groups, knowing very well that in some larger groups in the Institutes which have been running for years, real learning may have virtually ceased. (Southwark Institute of Adult Education, 1981: 23)

Other continuation strategies employed by the DfEE-supported demonstration outreach projects were:

● exploring whether discrete strands of a project (rather than the whole) might be taken over for funding by one of the current partners
● seeking opportunities to develop further the roles of groups and networks originally set up as part of the project
● encouraging volunteers to continue their own learning, thereby acting as informal ambassadors for learning in their community (some projects included incentives for future learning as part of the 'deal' with volunteers) (Watson and Tyers, 1998: 241)

One project sought to build sustainability for the future by adopting a 'cascade' model. Each volunteer was encouraged to run three presentations for their family, friends, neighbours and other contacts. Most of the attendees were non-learners for whom the intended outcome was a guidance interview or learning programme. In this way, the word was intended to be spread as widely as possible, using local 'ambassadors', rather than through the 'professionals'.

Conducting outreach activities with groups that are already established can also help to sustain work beyond the funding period. If completely new groups are formed to take part in educational outreach activities, the chances are that they will disperse when those activities come to an end. If the work is undertaken with an established group there is a better chance of its being taken forward and contributing to subsequent activities. According to a WEA officer: 'the best WEA practice is where education provision builds on other community activity such as tenants' issues, with tutors in a facilitating role'.

Capacity-building

The continuing tendency to fund community-based outreach work on a short-term basis suggests that developing local capacity should be a dominant aim of outreach. This requires outreach workers to identify and use the skills that already exist in the community:

> *There are real 'resource' people in the community who can relate to their neighbours and teach them a thing or two. They may not have strictly bona fide recognised educational qualifications, though they may have considerable industrial/commercial service experience over a number of years, and built up skills which they can share with other people.* (Southwark Institute, 1981: 23)

Training local people to promote and develop learning opportunities is an extremely effective means of community empowerment. As Portwood (1988) suggests, the best support outreach workers can provide at the end of a project is training to pass on their skills, knowledge and contacts. Watson and Tyers (1998) found that the typical outreach model, involving mainstream education or guidance providers taking their services out onto estates, achieves some success, but is resource-intensive and does little to encourage local communities to develop their own services. They believe that this can be better achieved by training volunteers as guidance workers in their own local communities:

> *For many projects, the pivotal task was recruiting and training local residents as volunteer information or guidance workers. These were to have an influence beyond the life of the project as local ambassadors or champions for learning. For many, training as a local guidance worker would become the first stage in a commitment to lifelong learning.* (Watson and Tyers, 1998: 230)

Supporting capacity-building, however, demands a certain humility on the part of education institutions which, in some cases, is difficult for them to demonstrate. As one outreach worker has found:

> *HE institutions and colleges are more affluent than community organisations and therefore have to be willing to do more than their primary function. FE sees their relationship with the community as very, very functional. Any capacity building they're doing is very much on these terms. But it should be an equal relationship.*

Reflecting on the projects involved in the NABCE programme in higher education, McNair (1999: 46-47) distinguished between those which focused on individual learners and their academic progression and those which focused on building community capacity. This 'collective' strand:

> *saw success in terms of the capacity of whole communities to engage with society, socially, politically and economically. It did not rest on linear notions of knowledge, and saw decisions about what is relevant knowledge as at least as much a matter for the community and learners as for academics....*
>
> *For work of this kind, the group was not an intermediary, assisting its members to climb onto a ladder, but was the location of learning. Its pedagogy was often based on the group, on collaborative ways of learning, and on using learning to address shared tasks. While it could be, and often was, the springboard for individual members to progress into the linear progression routes, this was not presented as its immediate or only purpose.*

McNair observes that division of the NABCE projects into these two categories has implications for funding methodology. As capacity-building is a long-term process which may not lead directly to enrolments in HE, it is difficult to support through the current funding methodology which is based on individual student numbers on mainstream programmes:

> *Many of those carrying out such work argued that one of the responsibilities of a higher education institution is to contribute to its communities, developing their economic and social capacity in a range of ways, of which the formal course is only one. Some of these activities may also take the form of outreach — community development work which is designed to change perceptions of the relevance of HE to community needs. A key feature of this work is that its impact is not adequately measured in terms of students enrolling on formal programmes* (McNair, 1999: 57)

McNair also notes that this kind of work can be expensive because it involves the development and maintenance of relationships with many agencies, and negotiation of educational activities which may not take the form of traditional courses. He argues that separate funding is required to support work that shares an institution's expertise, contributes to community capacity and addresses social exclusion. This should be flexible, ring-fenced, and sufficiently long-term to support the maintenance of partnerships with other agencies: 'many of which have been built over years, and are vulnerable to disruption from short-term funding programmes'. The new funding mechanism should:

- include strategies to conserve and make maximum use of the expertise of a relatively small body of staff, both full- and part-time
- reflect the fact that many potential participants cannot afford to pay

normal fees, despite the fact that the work may be relatively expensive in terms of staff, premises and equipment

- encourage innovation and flexibility, and take a broad view of 'higher' education, and not seek to narrowly exclude 'lower' levels of work.

McNair argues that such funding should not be based on a very narrow definition of higher education, short time-scales, or a too restrictive formula related to student numbers. Funds for community capacity-building should be allocated on the basis of agreed strategy and plans and subject to *post hoc* monitoring reports to the HEFCE, the institution's governing body and the local community.

However, the big question raised by the stress on community capacity-building in current policy is whether sufficient resources will actually be made available for it. A tariff-driven system which continues to give priority to student numbers and individual progression will support neither capacity-building nor the kind of painstaking outreach work that it requires:

A national tariff even with local variation is unlikely to offer a sufficiently flexible solution. The system must retain a capacity to adopt other creative mechanisms to achieve its ends (NIACE, 1999: 3)

If community regeneration and capacity-building are to be achieved in the areas that are most disadvantaged, then there will need to be dedicated budgets – both national and institutional – that are flexible enough to take account of community learning priorities. A recent consultation paper on post 16-funding (DfEE, 2000) does not emphasise either the assessment of community needs in making funding allocations or helping community groups and organisations access formula funds in order to build capacity. While there will be a block (10-15 per cent) of non-formula funding for the local Learning and Skills Council to use at their own discretion, adult and community learning will have to compete for a share of this with initiatives to do with workforce development and guidance as well as local regeneration initiatives and matched funding for European Social Fund and Single Regeneration Budget work. Welcome though it is, the non-formula funding element might also reinforce the marginalisation of outreach work in some organisations.

There needs therefore to be a rethink of current education funding in relation to lifelong learning and combating exclusion. If there is a genuine desire to widen participation in learning in disadvantaged communities, then there should be recognition of the implications of what this means in terms of sustained funding and support for outreach work.

CHAPTER SIX

The returns on investment in outreach

The Fryer report (1997: 21) refers to outreach and development work as 'often the vital prelude to eventually wider participation. Their precise outcomes may be difficult to calibrate but their general benefits are not at all to be doubted.'

What are these benefits and how can they be assessed? Do providers measure the returns on investment of resources and time in outreach? How can the effectiveness of outreach be demonstrated?

The evidence from the literature and current practice suggests that there are problems here, not least because of the different expectations and requirements of the three major stakeholders: community groups, funding bodies and education and training providers.

- Community groups want prompt responses to their learning needs and interests, access to resources and genuine partnership. However, the extent to which these can be achieved depends on the aims and decisions of other stakeholders.
- Funding bodies require fulfilment of contracts, value for money and achievement of targets such as increased numbers of learners and evidence of progression in terms of qualifications or movement into further education or employment. However, the complex nature of much outreach work is incompatible with the kind of economic indicators employed in funding systems:

The Treasury is always faced with choices between expenditures where the outcomes are incommensurable. Thus the discussion has to be conducted in money terms (real or financial). Problems inevitably arise in valuing outcomes....there is inevitably pressure to use simple indicators of 'performance' or 'value for money'. Such simple indicators inevitably fail to do justice to the complex phenomena they are intended to indicate....Improvements in quality and the valuation of new goods — innovations — have always caused measurement problems. Benefits which are widely diffused are hard to measure. Benefits which might be compounded with the effects of other variables will tend to be downplayed. Benefits which take time to arise will tend to be underestimated.
(Marquand, 1991)

Outreach activities are often innovative and experimental and hard, measurable outcomes may not be evident for some time. There is no way, for example, of assessing how valuable local contacts and networks are, and while it may be simple to count the number of people contacted and services provided, it is far more difficult to measure the impact of these on the attitudes, motivations and behaviour of targeted individuals and groups. Changes in attitudes and feelings are extremely difficult to quantify. In work with people with disabilities conducted by the University of Nottingham:

the most dramatic gains have been in self-confidence and self-esteem, as evidenced in the reports of the students themselves, their families and staff in the centres. However it is difficult to accredit such gains and justify such benefits to the relative funding bodies. Consequently this provision exists on uncertain, short-term project funding which inevitably limits its effectiveness. (HE Networks, 1999: 8)

- Education providers often want outreach to result in an increase in the numbers of participating students, greater interest in the programmes and courses they provide and evidence of educational progression. However, the effectiveness of outreach in terms of changing attitudes to education and increasing overall participation is also hard to assess, partly because of the time it may take before results may be seen, partly because of the difficulty of finding out what action has been taken in response to outreach activities.

You can talk to people and raise their awareness but it may be 6 weeks, 6 months, before they come back. That doesn't mean that there hasn't been a result only that results take time. Part of outreach brief is to make people aware of other opportunities, not just those offered by LEA, therefore it's a brokering process. But this part of the service isn't measurable because the learners won't necessarily come to us. (LEA outreach worker)

It is very difficult to track. When you think of how diverse our provision is and the range of avenues people can go down laterally or vertically. It's very hard to measure how effective you're being in reaching people because you only know about the ones you've got. (FE manager)

Student tracking between different organisations and institutions is notoriously difficult. In one of the DfEE demonstration projects (Watson and Tyers, 1998), attempts to track progress from initial enquiries to longer-term outcomes proved 'hugely challenging' because of difficulties with systems compatibility (different providers use different software for client records) and data protection (although individuals were willing to give their contact details to different providers, the latter were not able to pass them on to other providers without prior permission).

In some cases, of course, results *can* be measured in numbers, for example, when there are regular groups of people coming from an outreach learning situation into mainstream courses. At Northern College, group work is often a springboard for individual learning pathways. Groups start with bespoke courses and are then encouraged to attend the college and enter the accredited Pathways programme. Outreach work on estates in Hastings conducted by the University of Sussex has resulted in a number of people taking HE accredited courses. However, as McNair (1999: 9) points out, a lot of outreach and community development activity does not directly generate student numbers although there may be a long-term impact on patterns of participation in organised learning.

Moreover, educational outreach is often conducted with groups that are by definition hard to reach and who may need considerable support before they are able to participate in mainstream education and training. To demonstrate 'progression' among some of the most disadvantaged groups such as people with learning difficulties can be very difficult; not least because it cannot be measured in formal educational terms and may consist of very tiny steps: *Having to show progression is very difficult. The old FEFC question was: did each student learn something? Sometimes just moving a finger is evidence of progression for these students.* (FE Manager)

Outreach should therefore be considered as a long-term investment. However, not all providers are prepared to accept this. Several people engaged in doing or co-ordinating outreach work referred, during the course of this study, to difficulties they had experienced with persuading managers of the value of what they were doing:

Investment in outreach is quite high (premises/office, salaries, travel, phone, equipment) and we've had to struggle long and hard to convince people of the value of what we do. At one time we tried to cost the quality and quantity of contacts but this doesn't tell you much these are worth. (LEA outreach worker)

When the idea started it was passed over to the Enterprise Division whose aim was to make money for the college and the Head of Division was looking for cost-effectiveness. We've been threatened on and off with less money and less time for the project but the college now recognises the value of what we do and the Principal appreciates it. (FE outreach worker)

Evaluation of outreach activities

To identify these difficulties is not to imply that outreach work should *not* be rigorously evaluated and the outcomes assessed. Indeed, some feel that there has been too little monitoring of outreach work in the past and this has lessened its value and effectiveness:

Work deteriorated in 1980s because it was so vague. The results were nebulous and couldn't be evaluated. This is happening again. (HE practitioner)

No monitoring of outreach work ever took place. Consequently no new criteria for evaluating work was established to replace the rather crude one of numbers, except its hardly less subtle companion of numbers of the disadvantaged making it to mainstream classes....There was no mechanism set up for collating outreach work experience, or of drawing lessons from the success or failure of individual projects or initiatives for practice across London. (Taubman and Cushman, 1981: 45 and 47)

Moreover, as Gilman (1992: 49-50) points out, if you cannot show the value of outreach work it is unlikely that funding will be renewed:

Of the many reasons for evaluation perhaps the most often cited is that outreach projects are often only refundable subject to 'satisfactory evaluation'. In other words, outreach workers' jobs often depend upon evaluation. For this reason alone evaluation should be seen as integral to an outreach project right from the start.

Similarly, Watson and Tyers (1998) argue that the business case for future funding will be strengthened immeasurably by credible evidence that projects are making a difference. Other important reasons for continuous evaluation of outreach activities have been identified as the following:

- to identify and measure progress against original objectives and reformulate objectives where necessary
- to try to assess the returns on investment in outreach in order to make comparisons with other types of intervention
- to improve the effectiveness of outreach interventions
- to improve monitoring processes
- to record activities in order to share experience and allow comparisons with other outreach work. (Gilman, 1992)

Although it may take several years for outreach work to become properly established and produce the kind of results desired by funders and providers, regular evaluation processes should be in place from the start to demonstrate incremental progress towards agreed objectives. This, according to several outreach workers who reported to this study, means initial clarity of definition and purpose:

You need to define outreach first. If you don't define you can't outline criteria and if you don't outline aims and criteria, you can't assess success.

Work needs to be terribly specific with very specific aims. There have to be really clear criteria on which outreach is based.

Informants stressed that evaluation strategies should be built into the project design. Evaluation should be seen as a progressive and continuing process encompassing the whole outreach initiative and combining both quantitative and qualitative measures. Evaluation strategies should also be as flexible as the outreach strategies to which they are applied.

Evaluation methods

In their briefing based on the DfEE outreach demonstration projects, Watson and Tyers (1998) identified several methods that might be included in evaluation of this kind of work:

- researching local needs and recording the baseline position so that progress can be assessed over time
- recording progress on an ongoing basis (eg contacts made, training sessions given, perceptions of key players, feedback from participants, notes on events held)
- recording end-of-year or end-of-project position and comparing it with the baseline position. This would include management information and qualitative data (such as perceptions of key players including participants)
- synthesis of all information to assess progress and learning points.

Watson and Tyers argue that participant feedback is essential rather than an 'optional extra' in evaluation: outreach workers should collect both hard data (which is central to the business case for future funding) and participant feedback as this, especially if it leads to changes in activities and processes, encourages greater community trust and involvement.

The level of participant involvement in outreach activities is considered an important indicator of effectiveness by the DfEE (1999d) in the evaluation of work funded by the Adult and Community Learning Fund. One of the performance indicators the Department recommends for an interim evaluation of the fund was: *the extent of ownership of the learning process by the learners themselves and of active engagement in it.*

However, one of the problems with evaluating outreach activity in the past has been the lack of resources for recording and reflecting on the work. This is still often the case. Gilman (1992) suggests that one way of circumventing this problem is for supervision sessions involving outreach workers and managers to be routinely recorded. The information and data recorded can then be used both to monitor progress and to feed into interim and final reports. Other strategies involve a combination of internal and external evaluations.

At BBC Education, all Local Link Advisers meet regularly for sharing and feedback purposes and are encouraged to conduct evaluation meetings at the end of education campaigns. Independent research was also commissioned into the impact of the Learning Link Advisor scheme on intermediaries.

Benefits in relation to costs

Since outreach is largely seen as a process to help the most disadvantaged people engage in education, it is inevitably expensive. Work with people with literacy problems, limited formal education or learning difficulties may be particularly resource-intensive as tutors often have to work with very small groups. It is difficult to calculate the returns on such an investment since, as mentioned earlier, this kind of work is not susceptible to the kind of costing that is applied to more conventional, institution-based education provision. The DfEE (1999d) recognised this in their specification for evaluating the cost-effectiveness of the Adult and Community Learning Fund as a vehicle for delivering learning:

> 'Cost per unit' definitions {should be used} where and only where they make sense; and as far as feasible {provide} information to help the Department to analyse the relative costs of providing a given learning outcome through community-based provision and more conventional routes.

A (crude) way of calculating costs in relation to returns is to divide the budget allocated for outreach by the number of targeted students involved in any new activities generated. In one local authority area, this worked out at about £88 per student (although this sum would have increased if the outreach team had been expanded). However, if outreach activities are more concerned with guidance and raising awareness than with delivering programmes, it would obviously be harder to relate outcomes to costs unless the former applied only to the numbers of people reached and the number of enquiries generated.

In evaluating a TEC-funded outreach training scheme for disaffected youth, Perry (1996: 17-18) tried (not without difficulty) to do a cost-benefit analysis by dividing the total cost for all participants by the number of 'positive outcomes', and by dividing the total number of hours for all participants by the number of positive outcomes:

> It is important that some guide be obtained of the relative cost of positive outcomes as specified in the contract in order to ensure efficient use of future funding. The figure is gained from the number of positive outcomes divided by the income accrued through the hourly rate for all participants on the programme. However, he advised caution in interpreting the resulting figures: in implementing such an innovative programme the initial cost per positive outcome may vary due to differing circumstances between Centres and therefore caution should be applied in interpreting the results.

The method did nevertheless provide some useful statistics:

> In 1995 an overall target of 70% into education, training or work was contracted and 50% obtained within the first year which is very encouraging.

The target was arbitrary for this pilot but nevertheless proved a useful benchmark by which to gauge progress. Overall, in 1995 on average each positive outcome cost £254 to achieve, ranging from the lowest Centre at £28 with most falling in the £200-£300 range. Improvements to 1995 figures were made by most of the Centres from January to May 1996.

There were, however, (and this illustrates some of the problems identified in previous chapters), significant differences between the TEC and the contractor in their perception of what actually were positive outcomes:

The ethos, attitude, procedures and therefore outcomes of the Contractor were not in line with those of the TEC and the contract. There were substantial differences that made the programmes difficult to implement and difficult to monitor....The Contractor considered appropriate outcomes as far as they were concerned were the 'soft' outcomes of self-development, [and] thereafter the voluntary network, rather than the TEC 'hard' outcomes of training, education and employment. The Contractor focused on attending to the needs of the disaffected youth from a 'youth work' angle, selected the unemployed staff on these attitudes and supported them by reinforcing the messages throughout the programme. Outreach workers were therefore receiving conflicting messages from the Contractor and the TEC as well as being confused about the aims and objectives of the contract.

Views of what constitutes a successful outcome can depend on a person's work role: i.e. whether they are an outreach worker or a manager, as typified in a comment from a higher education manager:

X goes out and does wonderful work establishing the university's presence but if the measure of effectiveness is bums on seats then it's not very successful. He would say outreach is not about that, it's about empowerment and representing the university's presence but I disagree. It must be partly about that [recruitment].

Thus how people measure the impact of outreach activity and the return on investment in it depends largely on what they see as the aims of the work, for example whether it is seen as a capacity-building process for local groups or as a recruitment tool for the institution. A central aim of outreach at Northern College is capacity-building so 'success' is measured in relation to this: 'In the Dearne Valley we measured the impact by the number of new community organisations that came into existence as a result of outreach activities. This would be a basic measure of impact.' At BBC Education, each learning campaign has different objectives and is evaluated accordingly. Assessment of success might involve the number of people who watched a programme, sent for a pack, or engaged in a related learning session, as well as the number of local/regional partners involved in a specific campaign.

In one FE college, they use a 'business case' impact-assessment methodology that involves:

a cost-benefit analysis of every course or activity we do, on a case by case basis. It is not based on hard money. We have to analyse an activity according to its benefits both to the community and to us (e.g. progression through). All new courses are costed using a formula based on actual costs but financial loss is not a reason to not run it. We could cross-subsidise from other parts of the college. It's very difficult to work out exactly how much everything costs. We could quantify it but it would take forever. (College Manager)

The diversity of outreach activities and purposes and the range of possible outcomes suggest that there can be no single, hard and fast method of calculating costs and benefits. However, the helpful list of questions compiled by Sanderson *et al* (1998: 39) in their proposed tests for value-added might usefully be applied in doing a cost-benefit analysis of outreach:

Economy: how do actual costs compare with planned costs?
Efficiency: what is the relation of outputs to resource inputs?
Awareness: are intended beneficiaries aware of the service?
Take-up: are they actually receiving the service?
Quality: are quality standards and customer satisfaction being achieved?
Effectiveness: do actual outputs and outcomes achieve intended objectives?
Impact: what improvements are made to quality of community life?
Equity: is the distribution of outputs, outcomes, benefits and impact equitable?

The impact of outreach

There is already evidence that, when conducted in a sensitive and appropriate manner, outreach activities can have a significant impact:

1) on target groups and individuals

All the evidence shows that outreach can open up access to learning and stimulate demand for learning among people who do not habitually engage with organised education opportunities, although the time and effort involved in achieving this objective may be considerable:

Outcomes include quite large numbers of estate residents taking small steps such as attending a course that may or may not be work related, or attending sessions for which the main purpose was awareness raising (e.g. family workshops which gently introduced the idea of learning within the family). (Watson and Tyers 240)

There is little doubt that, in its broadest sense, outreach provision has contributed significantly to increasing participation in further education by individuals for whom local access was not previously an option. In relation to provision in the most excluded communities, whilst the number of participants forms a small proportion of the sector as a whole, this belies the extent of effort and investment made to attract new learners who have been hitherto disengaged from education and training. (FEFCW, 1999)

The kind of outcomes experienced by local people are illustrated in accounts of some of the projects funded under Project 99:

The Caffwood Centre in Bradford used their funding to provide short initiatives for residents on local estates, mainly families of white origin from severely socially disadvantaged backgrounds. Courses were all relevant to the needs of local people and included 'Get Crafty', providing the opportunity to learn and develop skills in decorating, painting, curtain-making and restoring dilapidated furniture, Community Sports Leadership training, Working with Citizens Course and a Positive Parenting Programme. 'The courses have given many people a new focus, a new direction in their lives, as well as enabling them to positively contribute to their community in the ways that these short term projects have enabled them to do…In particular the local school has benefited from the students running two sports clubs for the children during their lunch breaks and twice a week after school.'

Lancashire County Council used their funding to support the Clayton Brook Community Learning Project which has recently acquired a community house on the estate. Two workshops were facilitated on special paint effects and soft furnishings, the objective being to teach local volunteers new skills which would enable them participate in the refurbishment of the community house, as well as learning new ideas for their own homes. 'One young lady with no previous experience of sewing attended the soft furnishings workshop. Although at first somewhat hesitant and shy, she soon gained confidence as she leant new skills. By the end of the workshop she had learnt how to measure, cut out, use a sewing machine, and assemble curtains. She took a pair of curtains home to finish, proudly returning to present them to the house a few days later.' (Aldridge, 1999: 10)

2) on the wider community

The literature on educational outreach frequently reports net added value in terms of benefit to the community or locality although this may not be visible in the short term. Watson and Tyers (1998: 241) found that the work of many of the outreach demonstration projects was already having a lasting impact on the target communities through identifying needs that were met by previous provision. Among the examples they sited are:

the purchase or sharing of computer-aided guidance packages that will be available to the community beyond the funding period increasing the feeling of community on an estate, and developing informal networks amongst residents; the personal development of volunteers, including the facilitation of support groups; building up links with schools and agreeing to work collaboratively in the future to provide literacy classes for parents; establishing formal networks of contacts for community workers which raise morale and provide a framework for lobbying, information giving and acting as an intermediary to LEA provision.

The report of projects funded under Project 99 also includes examples of community outcomes, such as the one reported below:

The Global Community College received funding for outreach work to, and provision of taster sessions for, tenants' associations and local Agenda 21 environmental and community groups to help people identify needs, possible ways of addressing them and opportunities for learning how to deal with them. Five taster sessions were run, identifying themes such as: the issues raised by the 'Millennium Bug' and need for community preparedness as a social insurance policy, the need to use imaginative methods to make connections between local groups and international issues and decision-making processes; and the use of 'community visioning' as a way of involving stakeholders, building a shared vision and creating a plan of action for sustainable community development. (Aldridge, 1999: 14)

A study of informal community-based learning (McGivney, 1999) found evidence of an important 'ripple' effect from locally-based learning activities when, as educational outreach work became established in a number of deprived areas, the friends and families of initial participants started becoming involved.

During the course of this study, a county outreach co-ordinator described a similar process that occurred when one of the approaches she used led to a snowballing of recruitment:

One of the most successful methods I've used in 'virgin territory' was using questionnaires, a formal interview technique. People were pleased that someone wanted to know their opinion. From this I used a ' what do women want? approach with prior publicity. I got 24 people into a First Step course. The course was followed by one on assertiveness, then another Next Step, then another assertiveness. In the third year we were getting people from ABE who brought their family and friends along.

3) on providing organisations and institutions
Wherever possible, the impact of outreach activity on the providing organisation should also be evaluated. According to the account of outreach

activities conducted on the Aylesbury Estate, (Southwark Institute of AE, 1981), the long-term effects of interventions on the host institution should be evaluated in terms of '(a) the nature and extent of curriculum change; (b) the effect on full-time and part-time staff; (c) the involvement of ancillary staff; (d) the effect on in-service training, both in content and style; and (e) the resulting change in the composition of the student body'.

Some of the benefits of outreach activity for providers were identified during the course of this study as:

- recruitment of new learners to off-site and mainstream programmes
- the establishment of new networks and partnerships
- a higher profile and increased reputation in local communities
- generation of funds from other sources
- new demands on its services.

The need for a broad view of outcomes

Many analysts agree that there needs to be a broader view of what is meant by achievements than those currently prioritised by educational mainstream funding. As one practitioner commented: 'The only kind of achievement that government will accept is accreditation, but some of the ones used in the system are rubbish.' It is important for providers employing outreach activities to recognise that there are important outcomes beyond increased student recruitment and educational progression. If the latter are the only prized and recorded results, other arguably more worthwhile outcomes may not be recognised, as the following comments from staff at two FE colleges (see Chapter 2) indicate:

When we did nutrition for travellers only one went into FE but the kids' nutrition improved immeasurably.

A lot of local schools say that their Ofsted reports have been much better than expected. There are positive spin-offs from parents learning – it's cool to be in school. In a place like this where there are appalling GCSE rates, we need as many positive role models as possible. If you've got mum, auntie, brother or sister in long-term education and training, the impact is incalculable. If we didn't believe that we would have chopped it [outreach work] years ago because if you only take progression into account you'd obviously be making a loss.

These longer-term outcomes are incontestably more valuable than the number of adults who enrol in an institution's mainstream programmes which suggests that funders and institutions need to develop a broader and more flexible way of assessing returns on this kind of work. This requires a sea change in perspectives – a shift away from the continuing and disproportionate stress on individual progress towards an appreciation of the wider, collective, societal or community gains of outreach.

As Portwood (1988) and others argue, however, this requires: a significant degree of commitment from senior management in the allocation of resources; the adoption of 'a relatively unorthodox' style of pedagogy (which has implications for the appointment and training of staff); and a totally different conception of what constitutes 'success' so that participation in learning counts more than educational attainment. It also requires a considerable leap of faith on the part of funders – an acceptance that although it may take time for outreach to produce tangible results, it can have a significant pay-off in the long term. Thus outreach should be seen more as an investment than a cost.

CHAPTER SEVEN

Conclusions

This study has shown that, after a period in which outreach was accorded low priority, education providers are having to recover some of the concepts and practices involved in making an active engagement with their local communities. This process has been encouraged by a range of new policy and funding initiatives aimed at contributing to lifelong learning, assisting community regeneration and combating social exclusion. Outreaching is central to all these agendas and is particularly essential if lifelong learning is to become a reality and institutions are to meet widening participation targets.

The need to expand community-based learning activities has been a recurring theme of policy statements and documents. In her Foreword to the Adult and Community Fund Prospectus, Education and Employment Minister Baroness Blackstone stated:

We want to find new ways to invest in learning opportunities provided through grassroots, community-based activities which are familiar and relevant to people's everyday lives...We are convinced that people at local level know best what is needed and what will work for them. (DfEE, 1998b: 1)

The Report of the Policy Action Team on Skills (DfEE, 1999a: 13) also puts strong emphasis on first stage, community-based learning activities in which 'local people should, wherever possible, have a significant stake.' A number of the recommendations made in that report have been accepted by Government and are in various stages of implementation.

However, while policy documents frequently refer to outreach as a means of achieving locally-based learning, the main outreach strategy specified is through information and communications technologies (ICT) and the establishment of local learning centres offering access to ICT. The Government's response to the eighth report of the education and employment committee 1998-99, *Access for All?* states: 'we agree with the Committee about the importance of taking learning to people as much as taking people to learning' (Her Majesty's Government, 2000), but then refers largely to the University for Industry (UfI) and ICT as the means of doing this. Some believe that the post-16 education system is moving inexorably towards ICT as a means of delivering learning and widening participation in learning (see Oxtoby, 1999). Although ICT can be seen as a form of outreach, there is a danger of over-reliance on it as a means of reaching 'disadvantaged' populations and bridging the gap between those who engage in organised education and those who do not. While ICT-based learning can be delivered in diverse locations and therefore assist those who are geographically isolated or restricted in their mobility, it will not necessarily provide the vital social context that community-based learning requires – the building of relationships and development of informal, collective activities based on local priorities and needs.

The stress on the need for education providers to connect more with local communities is nevertheless very welcome and there is already evidence that the widening participation agenda is encouraging many to spread their nets more widely and extend their services into communities who are not taking advantage of mainstream provision. Despite ministerial appreciation of the link between local learning and community development, however, it is not clear in policy documents that the implications of doing the essential Outreach work that these processes entail have been fully understood and taken into consideration. There is an assumption, for example, that the word 'outreach' which is frequently mentioned as a means of reaching the socially excluded is readily understood and means the same to all people irrespective of their role and working environment. But, as any study of the subject quickly discovers, the term 'outreach' has acquired a variety of meanings when used in an educational context. It is variously defined as a concept, as any form of off-site provision, as a method of learning delivery, as a marketing and recruitment strategy, as a networking process, as a community support mechanism, as curriculum development, as a way or style of working, as a set of particular aims, and as a process involving a series of consecutive stages and activities.

In other words, 'outreach' has become an imprecise, catch-all term that tends to be applied to any activity that goes on outside the main buildings of an education institution or organisation. Currently the word is often used interchangeably with the terms 'widening participation' and 'combating exclusion' and it has become strongly connected with the notion of disadvantage. It has therefore acquired certain connotations that some dislike: namely, that is a branch of social work, providing assistance for poor and needy people; that it always involves low-level or remedial work; and that it entails the imposition of middle-class and institutional values and assumptions on working-class sections of the community – all of which imply an attitude of condescension. In consequence, some practitioners refuse to use the word at all, while others try to avoid these negative connotations by giving it a precise operational definition from the start. In many instances, however, the term is still used very loosely as though there were a universal understanding of the processes and aims of activities it implies. It is important, therefore, that policy makers and practitioners arrive at a shared meaning of what outreach is and the core concepts the word embraces.

The most common understanding of educational outreach is the mounting of activities outside centres and institutions, including (though not always) delivery of learning programmes, which are designed to connect with local communities and increase their awareness of and participation in different forms of organised education provision. However, there are differing views about the exact nature and purposes of this work.

Some institutional managers view it mainly as a tool for recruitment – as a means of increasing student numbers and gaining funding. Others view it as a means of empowering people by giving them opportunities to negotiate, plan and control the kinds of learning activities that will be of most relevance to them. According to this perspective, a principle of good outreach is that it should provide real benefits for all involved not just the benefits valued by funders and providers. The Policy Action Team on Skills (DfEE, 1999a) confirmed what community educators have known for decades – that people who have had poor school experiences and who see education institutions as remote and intimidating will only take advantage of learning opportunities which are both locally-based and have a strong connection with their lives and concerns. Although a legitimate role of outreach is to provide stepping stones to existing learning opportunities, many feel that it has a more important role in developing learning activities that are genuinely responsive to people's needs and which make a significant contribution to their lives:

Lifelong learning isn't more people doing the same things we have been doing every day. If it is we've failed'. (FE Manager)

If you push the social inclusion model then you have to get people engaged, You need to give them a stake in the system they're in. That's why outreach is so important if you want a cohesive, harmonious society. It can't just be an add-on extra; a special event odd people go on. (FE practitioner).

This interpretation of outreach puts learners at the centre. Outreach is construed not as a simple shifting of pre-packaged programmes from one location to another but as a process of consultation and consensus leading to joint planning of learning activities and programmes which are responsive to people's declared interests. This way outreach can contribute to the wider goals of lifelong learning as described by Fullick (1999: 5-6):

No amount of joined-up government thinking is a substitute for real strategies for lifelong learning which give people the skill and confidence to make sense of their present and define their own future. This means a lot more than old-style community education development work and will mean to go much wider and deeper. It will mean a change in culture where each individual is perceived as having the potential to learn from every situation and where the focus will be on developing personal capacities and learning relationships and networks which foster these capacities so that communities too can develop new ways of solving real problems....[We] need to empower people as stakeholders in their own communities.

This is the logical direction of outreach when it is seen in the wider context of community development and regeneration. Most formula funding, however, rewards education providers more for student recruitment and individual progression than for helping communities to embark on a process of positive change, and their responses to expressed learning demands are often constrained by the regulations that govern how they work and adherence to traditional institutional and power structures. This is a contradiction that remains unaddressed in policy:

> *Even when we try to work outside our institutional perspectives, the financial, procedural and political features of the institution limit what we can do. The best outreach work may develop subversive spaces, but in the end it will not transgress institutional expectations if initiative, funding and control is rooted in the centre.* (Stuart and Thomson 1995: 12)

Another assumption in policy is that adult, further and higher education providers have the capacity and expertise, as well as the motivation, to conduct the kind of work that will engage local people in learning. This prompts several questions: should all sectors engage in outreach or is it more appropriate for some sectors, areas and situations than others? Post-16 institutions have other agendas and priorities as well as inclusion and equity, and some feel that they are currently being pulled in all directions. Garrett (1999), for example, sees them as expected to be 'all things to all people'. He argues that clear sectoral differences should be maintained, and that, given their respective roles and expertise, the further education sector should do the initial contacting and first-stage provision in local areas, while higher education institutions should confine themselves to establishing a greater community presence and utilising local facilities to deliver courses:

> *Universities are being encouraged to produce both world class research and to undertake outreach work to those educationally disadvantaged in the locality. Colleges of FE are perhaps geared towards the latter over the former....It is not clear whether the future will see the majority of HEIs themselves conducting significant outreach work and offering considerable pre-higher education provision (as a few post 92 HEIs have done) or whether most HEIs will look to partnerships with local FE providers in the interests of widening participation. The latter course would be justified on the grounds that [colleges] offer a more diverse and well-rooted presence in the locality and greater expertise at pre-higher education provision (including basic skills work). This model appears more cogent in the interests of retaining some distinctions between the core missions of FE and HE. This not to say that HEIs shouldn't be concerned with widening participation but is to suggest that widening participation might be better served by HEIs utilising the expertise of FE rather than attempting to duplicate activity.*

Others analysts, however, worry that too much responsibility for widening participation among under-represented groups is being put on the further education sector and that this may result in colleges being perceived mainly as an educational route for less able learners:

> *The relationship between FE and the education and training system could be seen as one in which FE is being standardised to play an increased 'quantitative role' related to 'second chance populations' to complement other organisations which have more elite participants. Aspects of the New Deal would be an example of this....*
>
> *Colleges appear to be meant to cater for everyone, 16-19 year olds, both academic and vocational, adult returners, access students, HE students, those with special needs, the socially excluded and those not involved anywhere else....The virtue is increased commitment to access and achievement for all but the possible pitfalls are that FE lacks a clear strategic role either nationally or locally and is rather marginal to high prestige areas. There is a danger that in concentrating on basic skills and access, FE will fail to attract its fair share of faster more capable students.* (Green and Lucas, 1999 pp 29 and 35)

Here again, community-based work with different student populations is seen as automatically lower level, a perception reinforced by some current institutional practices. An FEFC inspector has typically found that widening participation work is often:

> *on the periphery – with low status teachers and learners. Many colleges will take you out to huts at the extreme ends of their campuses and that's where these people will be. Current initiatives are well meaning but they all leave the main frame in place.*

As with all forms of adult learning provision, however, the extent and quality of outreach is extremely variable and there are probably greater differences between individual institutions than between different sectors in the extent to which they conduct outreach activities. Some higher education institutions are more closely involved with their local communities than further education colleges (which is not surprising since, as Oxtoby (1999) asserts, many colleges have little in common with each other beyond 'their ability to change'). In some further education institutions, outreach is central to their mission; in others it is marginal – 'a separate and isolated process conducted in the margin by part-time staff with little institutional support, contact or power' (Johnston, 1986). In such cases, whatever the commitment of outreach workers, outreach efforts are unlikely to have much impact either on targeted communities or on institutional structures and practices. The work will continue to be perceived as lower level and therefore of lower priority.

The diversity of current practice prompts several questions: how does outreach fit with an institution's specific role? What kind of outreach activities should a specialist further education college or a Russell university conduct? What level of resources should institutions allocate to it? Where and at whom should efforts be targeted? These are complex questions which can create dilemmas for providing institutions, but which need to be addressed by every institution that is concerned with widening participation.

One could argue that all education providers have a role in contributing to lifelong learning and widening participation within their local communities, even if it is not their primary aim. It may be in their interests to do this especially if they want an increase in part-time students. Outreach work should therefore be viewed as part of the overall process of responding to adult learning requirements, although some feel that many institutions are not necessarily taking this on board. Ward and Steele (1999: 197-8), for example, argue that universities should take on a broader regional and local role, contributing to the development of local communities and the combating of poverty. Ward (1997) envisaged three models of institutional engagement with local communities (for HE). An economic benefit model with the university playing a key role as employer, landowner and investor in a regional or local economy; a community service model with local links established by student community action, community service initiatives and student placements; and a community development or empowerment model involving participatory research, educational development work and the development of strategic and democratic partnerships.

Whatever model of outreach is preferred, its impact and effectiveness will depend largely on the institutional commitment and resources dedicated to it.

The implications of doing outreach

It is clear from the literature and testimony of people working in the field that to make a genuine connection with local communities requires the full commitment of institutional managers, adequate resourcing and recognition of what embarking on such relationships entails. Outreach work should not involve the imposition of institutional (or personal) values and preferences, and providers should be prepared to respond, as far as they are able, to any new demands that may be generated by the dialogue between them and local communities:

> *It must be squarely faced that the exercise of going about interviewing people, explaining about the local adult education service, and asking them what they want, may result in them actually telling us!* (Southwark Institute of Adult Education, 1981: 21)

Outreach also means taking risks and allowing local groups to set their own agenda. As Education and Employment Secretary David Blunkett recently declared:

In building the capacity to regenerate confidence in providing social renewal, and in ensuring economic regeneration and employment, it must be the community itself that determines the direction. For far too long we have seen vast sums of central and local government funding pumped into programmes with which the local community had little affinity, and certainly no control....It is not merely that communities should have a say in how to spend national resources, or be consulted by outside professionals on the regeneration programmes – it is actually the community itself taking ownership of and determining the direction for that renewal programme, which will be crucial to success. In other words, we need 'to build from the bottom' so that local people have the chance to determine how and what will be successful for their area. This means taking risks, something which is seen as essential for economic enterprise and innovation in the business field, but must be now used in social policies. (Risk essential in making communities part of the solution for urban renewal, address at the Urban Renaissance conference, Balsall Heath, 9 May, 2000: Press Release 194/00).

Targeting

Exactly where and on whom to focus outreach activities is a key initial question for providers. It may be impossible to cover whole geographical areas and populations, so difficult choices may have to be made. If funding is available for work in specific priority areas, institutions will understandably be tempted to locate some of their outreach work there. A problem identified during this study was that some priority zones have been attracting the lion's share of regeneration money, with the result that community-based initiatives have been concentrated in these locations without proper co-ordination or connection. This has sometimes led to duplication and conflicts with other agencies and providers working in the same area and with the same people. It has also meant that other areas which have pockets of similar deprivation, but which are less visible and fashionable in funding terms, have been neglected.

If an institution decides to target outreach at particular groups, it may face a similar dilemma. Targeting those who fall into neat categories defined by a single characteristic – lone parents and the unemployed – may make outreach efforts more manageable but can leave some groups unprovided for and divert attention from the need to create a fairer and more inclusive overall post-16 system. As Meagher (1999: 303) argues, it can also disguise the deeper causes of poverty, with the real problems of social inequalities ignored:

There is a tendency...to treat people as if they should or could fit into neatly defined and discrete categories such as 'ethnic minorities' 'women' 'disabled' or 'disadvantaged' – ignoring the fact that their everyday lived experience does not fit neatly into the convenient funding or policy categories we create for them. Moreover there is a real danger that an uncritical acceptance of such 'category politics' encourages the postmodernist emphasis on diversity and difference at the expense of a class analysis as a way of explaining a system that creates and sustains deep inequalities within our society....In this context, it is easy to see how category politics of this kind can be used to legitimate a trend in policy that moves away from the provision of good, accessible, universal services towards one that develops selective services for specific groups – and is cheaper for increasingly cash starved local government to provide.

...It is far easier to seek comfort in parcelling out bits of equality in opportunity – not of outcome – to groups who can safely be accommodated in mainstream provision.

Even when 'disadvantage' is used as a criterion for selection of target groups (which it usually is), it is often, as ILEA outreach workers found 20 years ago, the more easily reached and 'acceptable' groups which are contacted:

If we are genuinely assessing priority needs in different geographical areas of Inner London, why do we all come up with such similar formulae – e.g. activities for mothers and toddlers? (Nicholls and Murray, 1981: 60)

Recent research into the kinds of outreach activity being conducted by colleges in Wales found:

lots of activity, but it is not necessarily successfully reaching the hardest to reach groups, and this is where there is a need for steerage. One practitioner has informed me of a tendency to 'recycle' old learners for new outreach initiatives, which gives the impression that we are widening participation when we are not.

If social, economic and educational disadvantage are to govern choices of who to work with, then institutions need to carry out thorough preliminary local research in order to identify the areas and groups least provided for, not just select these from a predetermined list.

The frequency with which the word outreach is invoked in policy documents as a means of meeting the social inclusion agenda without qualifying clauses or caveats assumes that it is a straightforward process. This study demonstrated that, on the contrary, it is an exceedingly complex and exacting process.

Moreover, the current connection of educational outreach with the notion of disadvantage has fuelled the belief that outreach work is automatically low level, or, as suggested above, 'for second chance populations'. It is not, although some institutions reinforce this view by only doing low-level or remedial (basic skills), locally-based work. All the evidence suggests that in order to create a more inclusive adult education system in learning, outreach work should be disentangled from the notion of disadvantage. It should be integral and complementary to, and have parity of esteem with, the mainstream work of a providing organisation institution. One informant described the post-16 system as: 'a tartan cloth in which the different strands of colour represent different types of student but each is as important as the other: no strand is the fringe hanging off the end.'

Investing in people

The success of any outreach venture ultimately depends on the personality and capabilities of the workers who do it: they are, as one informant to this study argued, the 'key link in the chain'. A recent study of informal learning (McGivney, 1999) showed that the most important factor in encouraging people to engage in and continue learning is the influence of 'key' persons – outreach development or guidance workers, primary health workers, community leaders, local 'opinion leaders' – people who inform, encourage, advise and support individuals and groups and act as intermediaries between them and education providers. Thus widening participation in learning among the most disadvantaged sections of society can be achieved by investing in the people with the necessary skills in networking and conducting the essential development work in different communities. This kind of work is labour-intensive and time-consuming and, for it to be effective, staff require adequate time and funding as well as an employment status that signals that they are central not marginal workers.

In many if not most providing institutions, however, outreach workers are employed on part-time and temporary contracts and occupy an ambivalent position in relation to their institution-based colleagues. Given the importance of outreach to lifelong learning and community regeneration, its demanding nature should be recognised and staff appointed on terms and conditions commensurate with the responsibilities it involves. People engaged in this capacity should not always be on short-term contracts but should enjoy terms and conditions of employment that are on a par with institution-based staff. Outreach activities should also be part of overall institutional responsibility rather than one person's role. As one FE informant pointed out: 'If you label a staff member just according to a certain concept you marginalise them.'

This study has confirmed that groundwork such as networking in the community requires a complex tapestry of skills. Since many of the people with the necessary experience have left the education sector in recent years, relevant staff development should be provided for those who are new to this kind of work. Even if outreach entails no more than off-site delivery of programmes, people used to working only in institutional environments cannot be expected to work in community venues without some training or preparation. New outreach workers may also require help to develop the broader skills required in community liaison and networking. Several people who reported to this study stressed the need for an accredited national training programme that would cover the core skills needed in outreach.

Such a programme could perhaps be developed in collaboration with sectors such as youth and community work in which outreach is an essential and well-established dimension of core activities.

Support for outreach

The extent to which education institutions engage in community-based work is to a large extent driven by what one informant referred to as the 'two big levers' – funding and inspection and the criteria and targets these impose.

If widening participation is the business of all post 16 providers, and if they are expected to fulfil the greater community role that is expected of them, then there has to be a consideration of how this is to be supported. Outreach activities are extremely time-consuming and resource-intensive and the flexibility that is their hallmark is incompatible with current mainstream funding regimes. There needs, therefore, to be some re-examination of funding for this work. On the one hand locally-based and locally-inspired work is being strongly encouraged; on the other it is routinely undervalued and under-supported. This contradiction needs to be addressed. Although there are some pots of funding available for community-based work, these are often short-term and distributed on a competitive basis. The study highlighted the perennially familiar problems arising from short-term finance: the work is seen as low priority; it may disappear at the end of the funding term without major or long-term impact; staff may find other jobs leading to lack of continuity; the work may raise expectations that cannot be met, and too short an engagement can lead to loss of trust and damage the credibility of providers. There is also the built-in contradiction that funders often expect long-term results from short-term resourcing and may use the failure to deliver these as a reason for not continuing to support outreach and development work. This is despite substantial evidence that changing long-established attitudes, values and behaviour is a very long-term process: 'If long-term projects are not encouraged more strongly how can long-term benefit be expected from the community?' (Fremeaux, 2000: 66).

As an instrument for widening participation in learning and assisting community generation, outreach must be seen as a long-term project. It therefore needs to be supported in a way that takes into account that outcomes, in terms of visible changes in attitude and behaviour, are more likely to be seen in the long rather than short term. There should therefore be dedicated budgets – both national and institutional – that are flexible enough to allow realistic time-scales for the necessary development work to take place before outputs are required, and which recognise this kind of work as a long-term investment rather than an add-on cost. To maintain their community-based work, institutions should allocate a certain percentage of their central resources specifically to outreach and should be monitored to ensure that this does not get absorbed by other areas of work perceived to be of greater and more immediate priority:

> *Development work requires resources to build relationships, to plan and design new approaches, materials and programmes. This can be done at national level or by institutions top-slicing budgets to create specific funds for this purpose. Creating a ring-fenced fund for development work, both nationally and within an institution, can be important in maintaining its priority. Without it other priorities can suck the resource away, and undermine the work* (McNair, 1999: 65)

There are some welcome developments in the new funding proposals contained in the Learning and Skills Bill and first technical consultation paper on funding allocations (DfEE, 2000). In the new funding model introduced by the Bill, the eligibility of the learner rather than what is learned will be key, and new learners from under-represented groups will be 'unit rich'. According to a further education informant: 'If you're a new learner you should get more funding than someone already benefiting from the system.' Another welcome development is the proposal to make some non-formula funding available to the 47 Local Learning and Skills Councils (LLSCs) for some adult and community learning as well as other things such as guidance, workforce development, widening participation and local regeneration initiatives. However, there are dangers here: the funds are expected to cover so many areas that community-based learning may be overlooked. The LLSCs will inevitably have different priorities and leaving the allocation of such funds to their discretion could lead to a continuation of the wide geographical discrepancies that have long characterised adult and community learning provision in the UK. Moreover, non-formula funding could reinforce marginalisation.

There is also a question about whether the local councils will be able to design and deliver services that are truly responsive to local circumstances and needs since neither the process of community needs assessment not the vital role of community and voluntary organisations in building capacity through learning have been fully taken into account in the new funding proposals. Some also worry that smaller voluntary organisations will be not be represented on the local councils.

It has long been recognised that the voluntary sector makes a vital contribution to increasing participation in learning:

> *It would seem to be in the general public interest for the experience, power and resources of the statutory bodies to be united with the vitality, commitment and expertise of the voluntary sector in pursuit of the common goal of providing rich and varied educational opportunities for adults in the community.* (McGivney, 1986: 33)

The experience and capacity of the voluntary sector in working with disadvantaged sections of the population is frequently acknowledged in policy documents. Paragraph 3.16 of the Learning and Skills Council Prospectus states: 'it will be important to ensure that LSC funding is accessible to community and voluntary organisations, who are best-placed to provide learning in the most socially disadvantaged communities'. (DfEE, 1999c).

It is to be noted, however, that there has been far more emphasis on the business community than on the voluntary sector in the criteria for the composition of the Local Learning and Skills Councils. One of the most interesting and potentially most effective outreach activities currently being conducted by education providers is the training of local people to become learning champions, signposters or animateurs in their own communities. This is the kind of work that should be supported by the LLSCs and other funding bodies if there is a genuine wish to involve excluded groups in learning and encourage community regeneration. But it will require close collaboration with the voluntary sector.

There is also a question about what the LLSCs will regard, for funding purposes, as the most valuable learning outcomes and achievements. There is a danger that these may continue to be viewed narrowly as employment or qualifications whereas the outcomes of outreach activities may be infinitely broader than these. Cost-benefit analyses that only take into account student numbers, educational progression and employment outcomes may fail to recognise that there are sometimes far more valuable gains for the wider community, as two further education colleges have found:

When we did Nutrition for Travellers only one went into FE, but the kids' nutrition improved immeasurably.

A lot of local schools say that their Ofsted reports have been much better than expected. There are positive spin-offs from parents learning.

Achievements such as these should be recognised and celebrated. They are what outreach should be all about.

References

Aldridge F, *Short and Sweet*, NIACE, 1999

Brent J and Brent M, *Outreach work in the youth and community service*, London Borough of Hounslow Youth and Community Service, 1992

Brookfield S, *Adult learners, adult education and the community*, Open University Press, 1983

Charnley A and Withnall A, *Developments in Basic Education: special development projects 1978-85*, ALBSU, 1989

Clancy K and Stuart M, 'Who is the tutor? Housebound learning programmes' in Stuart M and Thomson A (eds), *Engaging with difference: the 'other' in adult education*, pp 50-64, 1995

Clark D, 'Education for Community in the 1990s: a Christian perspective' in Allen G and Martin I (eds), *Education and Community: the politics of practice*, Cassell, pp. 118-129, 1992

Clarke K and Taubman D, 'A proposal for the appointment of secondary staff to advisory teacher posts for community (outreach) education' in Southwark Institute of Adult Education (ILEA), *The Aylesbury Estate: an action research project on Aylesbury Estate*, pp. 50-55, 1981. (Republished in 2000 by NIACE as *Aylesbury Revisited: Outreach in the 1980s*)

Department for Education and Employment, *The Learning Age. A Renaissance for a New Britain*, The Stationery Office, 1998a

Department for Education and Employment, *Adult and Community Learning Fund: Prospectus*, 1998b

Department for Education and Employment, *Skills for neighbourhood renewal: local solutions*, the report of the Policy Action Team on Skills, 1999a

Department for Education and Employment, *Learning to Succeed: A new framework for post-16 learning*, 1999b

Department for Education and Employment, *The Learning and Skills Council Prospectus: Learning to Succeed*, 1999c

Department for Education and Employment, *Specification for an Interim Evaluation of the Adult and Community Learning Fund*, DfEE, 1999d

Department for Education and Employment, *Learning to Succeed Post 16 Funding and Allocations: first technical consultation paper*, 2000

Department of Education and Science, *Adult Education: A plan for development* (Russell Report), HMSO, 1973

Diamond J, 'Access Year 2000 and Beyond – what next?' *Adults Learning*, 11/4 December, pp. 18-20, 1999

Dinsdale J, *Working in Widening Participation*, Queen Mary and Westfield College, University of London, 1999

Dowding J, 'Women's Education Development Project in Refuges and Hostels' in WEA, *Best Practice: effective teaching and learning in WEA courses and projects*, National Association, p. 45, 1999

FEU/REPLAN, *The Outreach College*, pp. 12-14, 1990a

FEU/REPLAN, 'Drawing on Experience', *REPLAN Projects Review*, 1990b

Ford G and Jackson H, *The WEA and Partnerships*, WEA National Association, pp. 4-7, 1999

Fordham P, Poulton G and Randle L, *Learning Networks in Adult Education: non-formal education on a housing estate*, Routledge & Kegan Paul, 1979

Francis H, *Wales a learning country: the 1999 handbook for lifelong learning*, University of Wales Swansea, Centre for Lifelong Learning, 1999

Fremeaux I, 'Community and Cultural Policy: the Arts Worldwide Bangladeshi Festival', *Rising East: the journal of East London Studies*, 3/3, pp. 46-68, 2000

Fryer R H, *Learning for the 21st Century.* First Report of the National Advisory Group for Continuing Education and Lifelong Learning, HMSO, 1997

Fullick L, *Lifelong Learning, social inclusion and social change*, second Philip Jones Memorial Lecture, NIACE, 1999

Further Education Funding Council (Wales), *Bulletin: Further Education Outreach Provision in Wales*, FEFCW, 1999

Garrett R, *Widening Access and Participation in Higher Education*, Report of the APT Project (Access and Participation Together), University of Surrey, School of Education Studies, pp. 40-46, 1999

Gilman M, *Outreach: Drugs Work: 2*, Institute for the Study of Drug Dependence, 1992

Green A and Lucas N (eds), *Further Education and Lifelong Learning: Realigning the sector for the 21st century*, Bedford Way Papers, University of London, Institute of Education, 1999

Her Majesty's Government, *Government's response to the 8th Report of the Education and Employment Committee 1998-99, Annex A to Select Committee on Education and Employment First Special Report: Access for all? A survey of post 16 participation* (9th Feb, House of Commons), 2000

Higher Education Funding Council (England) (HEFCE), *Widening Participation in Higher Education Funding Decisions*, Report, April 99/24, 1999

Higher Education Networks, *Update on Inclusion: widening participation in Higher Education*, Issue 1 Spring, p8, 1999

Johnston R, 'Outreach work: Principles and policy', *REPLAN ISSUES 1*, 1986

Johnston R, 'Education and unwaged adults: relevance, social control and empowerment' in Allen G and Martin I (eds), *Education and Community: the politics of practice*, Cassell, pp. 66-76, 1992

Kennedy H, QC, *Learning Works: Widening participation in further education*, Further Education Funding Council, 1997

Kinneavy T, *The Outreach College: design and implementation*, FEU/REPLAN, 1989

Mace J, *Talking about literacy: principles and practice of adult literacy education*, Routledge, 1992

MacSween K A, *An evaluative report on the rural outreach pilot service*, Berkshire Local Authority (Sexual Health and Educational Needs of Young People in West Berkshire), 1993

Marquand J, 'Training policy and economic theory: a policy-maker's perspective', paper presented at 'The International Conference on the Economics of Training. Differing Perspectives on Theory, Methodology and Policy', Cardiff, 1981

Martin I, 'Community education: LEAs and the dilemma of individualism' in Allen G and Martin I (eds), *Education and Community: the politics of practice*, Cassell, pp. 28-33, 1992

McGivney V, *Voluntary-Statutory Partnerships in the Education of Adults*, Unit for the Development of Adult Continuing Education, 1986

McGivney V, *Informal learning in the Community: a trigger for change and development*, NIACE, 1999

McGivney V, *Working with Excluded Groups: guidelines on good practice for providers and policy makers in working with groups under-represented in adult learning*, NIACE/ Oxfordshire Strategic Partnership, 2000

McNair S with Cara S, McGivney V, Raybould F, Soulsby J, Thomson A and Vaughan M, *Non Award-Bearing Continuing Education*, NIACE, 1999

Meagher J, 'Equal opportunities: Back to basics' in Crowther J, Martin I and Shaw M (eds), *Popular education and social movements in Scotland today*, NIACE, pp. 300-304, 1999

Ministry of Housing and Local Government, *People and Planning*, report of the Committee on Public Participation in Planning (The Skeffington Report), HMSO, 1969

Moser Sir C, *Improving Literacy and Numeracy: A Fresh Start*, DfEE, 2000

Nash I, 'Go Local for Learning', *Times Educational Supplement*, 23 July 1999, p39

NIACE, *A NIACE briefing on post 16 education and training: anticipating the legislation*, All Party Parliamentary Group on Adult Learning, 1999

NIACE, 'The increase in the learning divide', *Adults Learning*, 11/10, June, 12-13, 2000

Nicholls S and Murray E, 'The unease of the outreach workers', Associated papers, in Southwark Institute of Adult Education, *The Aylesbury Estate: an action research project on Aylesbury Estate*, pp 56-62, 1981. (Republished in 2000 by NIACE as *Aylesbury Revisited: Outreach in the 1980s)*

Organisation for Economic Co-operation and Development (OECD), *Lifelong Learning for all*, Paris: OECD, 1996

Organisation for Economic Co-operation and Development (OECD), *Overcoming Exclusion through Adult Learning*, Centre for Educational Research and Innovation, Paris, 1999

Oxtoby B, 'What will Further Education Colleges be like in 2015?', *Viewpoint, Education and Training*, 41/9, pp. 396-401, 1999

Perry T, *The disaffected youth project: evaluation, impact and effectiveness of outreach provision*, Status A Report, South Glamorgan TEC, 1996

Portwood D, *Outreach and Inreach: colleges and unemployment groups*, FEU REPLAN, 1988

REPLAN, *Review No. 1*, Department of Education and Science, 1986

REPLAN South and South West, *Reaching Out: further education and work in and with the community*, Resources, 1989

REPLAN South West Resources, *Outreach*, REPLAN ISSUES 1, NIACE, 1990

Rhodes T and Stimson G, *Buzzwords: an HIV Outreach Glossary*, Druglink, January/ February, pp. 8-10, 1994

Sanderson I *et al*, *Made to Measure: evaluation in practice in local government*, Local Government Training Board, London, quoted in DfEE, undated, Practice Progress and Value: learning communities: assessing the value they add, DfEE/NIACE, p. 39, 1998

The Scottish Office, *Lifelong Learning in the Community*, Liaise (Learning Initiatives for Adults in Scottish Education) Edinburgh, 1996

The Scottish Office, *Communities Change through Learning*, report of the Working Group on the Future of Community Education, Edinburgh, 1998

Sharma J and Selway I, 'Digestible, bite-sized learning opportunities for the learning age', *Face to Face, Forum for the Advancement of Continuing Education*, issue 14, February 10-13, 2000

Smith M K, *Local education: community, conversation, praxis*, Milton Keynes, Open University Press, 1994

The Social Exclusion Unit, *Bringing Britain Together: a national strategy for neighbourhood renewal*, 1999

Soulsby J, 'Rural older learners', *Ad Lib* (Journal for Continuing Liberal Adult Education), Issue 13, November, pp. 7-9, 1999

Southwark Institute of Adult Education (ILEA), *The Aylesbury Estate: an action research project on Aylesbury Estate*, ILEA, 1981. (Republished in 2000 by NIACE as *Aylesbury Revisited: Outreach in the 1980s*)

Steele T, 'With real feeling and just sense: rehistoricising popular education' in Crowther J, Martin I and Shaw M (eds), *Popular education and social movements in Scotland today*, NIACE, pp. 95-105, 1999

Stewart J, *Institutional Outreach in Adult and Community Education: ragged around the edges*, Report for the Commonwealth Relations Trust, 1995

Stuart M, 'Education and self identity: a process of inclusion and exclusion' in Stuart M and Thomson A (eds), *Engaging with difference: the 'other' in adult education*, 1995

Stuart M and Thomson A (eds), *Engaging with difference: the 'other' in adult education*, 1995

Taubman D and Cushman M, 'A history of ILEA outreach work and its precursors' in Southwark Institute of Adult Education, *The Aylesbury Estate: an action research project on Aylesbury Estate*, pp. 39-49, 1981. (Republished in 2000 by NIACE as *Aylesbury Revisited: Outreach in the 1980s*)

Taylor J, 'A long-standing struggle', *Adults Learning*, 11/6, December, pp. 17-19, 2000

Tidswell A and Warrender J, 'Opening the doors', *Adults Learning*, 112, pp. 10-11, 1999

Trotman C and Pudner H, 'What's the point? Questions that matter in community-based projects designed to counter social exclusion and increase participation in continuing education' in Preece J (ed) with Weatherald C and Woodrow M, *Beyond the Boundaries: exploring the potential of widening provision in higher education*, pp. 50-55, 1998

Uden T, *Widening Participation: routes to a learning society*, a policy discussion paper, NIACE, 1996

Ward K, *Replan Review 1*, August, Department of Education and Science, 1986

Ward K, 'Community regeneration and social exclusion: some current policy issues for H.E.' in Elliott J *et al* (eds), *Universities and their Communities*, Lawrence and Wishart, 1997

Ward K and Steele T, 'From marginality to expansion: an overview of recent trends and developments in widening p in England and Scotland', *Journal of Access and Credit Studies* Vol 1 No 2, pp. 192-203, 1999

Watson A and Tyers C, *Demonstration Outreach Projects: identification of good practice*, Final Report, National overview with individual project reports, SWA Consulting, 1998

WEA, *Best Practice: effective teaching and learning in WEA courses and projects*, National Association, 1999

Weatherald C and Layer G, 'As broad as it's long: challenging the limitations of traditional continuing education strategies for widening participation' in Preece J (ed), *Beyond the Boundaries: exploring the potential of widening provision in higher education*, pp 56-64, 1998

Wood A, *Oxfordshire County Council Lifelong Learning Outreach Strategy*, Oxfordshire County Council, October, 1999

Wood A, *A Guide to Outreach with Laptops*, NIACE, 2000